Looking *for* Wales

For friends beyond Offa's Dyke –

Nick and Sue,
and for Colin

Looking for **Wales**

An introductory guide

GERALD MORGAN

First impression: 2013
© Gerald Morgan & Y Lolfa Cyf., 2013

This book is subject to copyright and may not be reproduced
by any means except for review purposeswithout the prior
written consent of the publishers.

The publishers with to acknowledge the support
of Cyngor Llyfrau Cymru

Cover design: Y Lolfa

ISBN: 978-1-84771-707-8

Published and printed in Wales
on paper from well managed forests by
Y Lolfa Cyf., Talybont, Ceredigion SY24 5HE
e-mail ylolfa@ylolfa.com
website www.ylolfa.com
tel. 01970 832 304
fax 832 782

Contents

Acknowledgments

Never apologise, they say – but I must. I was asked by the publisher for a rather different book about Wales. Nevertheless, when I offered this to him, he graciously accepted. It's not a volume of profound research, but it contains some good stories, which I have done my best to make attractive to the reader. You may think you can survive without knowing about Winston Churchill and the Welsh goat, about Paulo Radmilović, Edith Mair Leonard, John Graham Chambers or Samothes. I would like to persuade you otherwise.

My warm thanks to Cynog Dafis, Dr Karen Jankulak, Thomas Lloyd, Dr Katharine Olson, Professor J. Beverley Smith, David Stephenson who gave me advice, and to Professor Laura McAllister and Mari Wyn of SportWales, Helen Bushell of the Welsh Hockey Union, Louise Carter of the Welsh Netball Association. I am also indebted to my sons Rhys, Geraint and Deiniol and to my wife Enid, who have all helped with various aspects of this book. I alone am responsible for any errors. Special thanks to the staff of Gwasg y Lolfa.

Gerald Morgan
Aberystwyth

1. Looking *for* Welsh Icons

Dragons

Every nation has its icons, or if you prefer, its symbols of identity. They appear on flags and badges, on paper and on screens, carved into monuments and sold by the thousand as cuddly toys. Many such icons are creatures or plants, whether the kiwi, the springbok, the wallaby of the southern hemisphere or the maple leaf, thistle and the shamrock in the north. Some icons have become abominable by association; thus the swastika was a perfectly acceptable artistic symbol for millennia until adopted as the badge of the Third Reich. For a small country Wales has a remarkable number of icons, some older than others.

Looking for dragons? Just look around. You don't have to go far to find red dragons – indeed you can't avoid them in modern Wales. It's not just the flags on public buildings and in people's front gardens. It's not just the road-signs at the border. It's not just the sports pages of the *Western Mail* and indeed of London newspapers, though they do love the beast. The Dragon Roars, the Dragon Breathes Fire when Wales wins, the Dragon Wilts when Wales loses.

Look in the commercial section of any Welsh telephone directory. The mid Wales volume lists eleven Dragons. They include Dragon Gates and Electrical Automated Gates and Barriers, Dragon Phoenix Takeaways (an odd combination, that; I wouldn't want to eat either, let alone both), Dragon Print, Dragon River Ltd and a Chinese takeaway, Dragons' Lair – of course the Chinese have an even more ancient right to the dragon than the Welsh, but the *red* dragon is ours. Dragons have been used to sell butter, lamb, leather goods, beer and world travel. Then of course there are sports teams, like the Gwent Dragons rugby club or the Celtic Dragons netball team.

The dragon is a strange icon for a tiny country where, although Milton described Wales as 'an old and haughty Nation, proud in arms', the fierce riots of the 19th century were countered by an anxious cult of Respectability. The English, as martial a nation as any, cultivate the lovely rose and the fighting Irish flaunt the lilting harp as well as the humble shamrock. Only the Scots thistle competes with the dragon for metaphorical menace.

The earliest appearance of the Welsh dragon is in the legend of the battle of the red and white dragons. The tenth-century Latin document called *The History of the Britons* tells the story of Vortigern and his betrayal of the British race to the Saxons. He then escaped from southern Britain to Gwynedd and tried to build a fortress on the great crag of Dinas Emrys, north-east of Beddgelert. The foundations kept collapsing, and when the wonder-child Emrys was brought in he explained what was happening: the castle could not be built because a red and a white dragon were fighting in a pool in the bowels of the rock. The red represented Wales, the white, England. Often it seemed that the white dragon was winning, but eventually – so he prophesied – the red will drive out the white. This almost happened, the author tells us, but unfortunately the many sins of the British meant that the Saxons have so far triumphed over them.

Pursuit of the Welsh red dragon further back than the tenth century is impossible, but Roman soldiers certainly brought the dragon image to Britain. During their occupation British people made brooches and pins with a dragon motif, and the monster must have remained here in the dark abysm of time after the Roman departure; Welsh *draig* derives directly from Latin *draco*, and must have been borrowed before the end of the Roman occupation. Certainly the poets of the Welsh princes rejoiced in the creature, time and again telling audiences how their patrons resembled both the fearsome dragon and the lion (Welsh *llew*). The most striking reference is in the magnificent elegy to Llywelyn ap Gruffudd after his death in 1282. The poet is elegising the prince's head, struck off for display in London: *Pen dragon, pen draig oedd arno*. It's a tough line to translate, since Welsh allows both *dragon* and *draig* where English has only the one word, and the line is metaphorical. The main point is that the poet and his audience knew Geoffrey of Monmouth's elaboration of the Arthurian legend in his *History of the Kings of Britain*. His hearers would have been aware firstly, of the title *pen dragon* as the name of Arthur's father Uthr Pendragon, and secondly, where *pen draig* means literally, 'he had a dragon's head', the poet clearly refers to the dragon-crested helmet worn by Arthur in Geoffrey's story.

The white and red dragon legend figures are also mentioned in Geoffrey's *Historia*, which was read all over western Europe and widely translated; there are three different translations in Welsh alone. It figures in the Welsh medieval tale *Lludd and Llefelys*, and in the Welsh Triads. The burial of the two dragons was one of the three fortunate concealments of the Island of Britain, and their disinterment one of the three unfortunate disclosures, since it led to renewed warfare between Welsh and English.

The Welsh had no monopoly of dragons in medieval Europe; Harold of England sported a dragon banner at the battle of Hastings. The Normans ignored the symbol, but with the spread of the legend of Arthur, king of Britain and wearer of a dragon-crested helmet, both Richard I and his brother John made use of the dragon as a propaganda device. Incidentally perhaps they hoped to promote Welsh sympathy as a by-product. Henry III's army even bore a red dragon symbol when defeating the Welsh in 1245, but after Henry's time the English became enamoured of the mythical St George and his cross. The Welsh princes themselves didn't use the dragon as a heraldic symbol; the shield of the princes of Gwynedd bore four lions.

References to the red dragon of Wales in later medieval poetry are rather scarce, and usually refer back to the Dinas Emrys legend without any more interesting significance. Several, however, are more meaningful. In 1378 the last male descendant in the direct line of the princes of Gwynedd, Owain Lawgoch, sought to recover his princedom with French help, and the poets looked forward eagerly to his coming. One of them connected Owain with the Dinas Emrys legend:

> This is the year, quite surely,
> When the white dragon will flee,
> And the red dragon, on the path of wrath,
> Bearing its flame, will crush it.

Welsh poets had looked to Owain, murdered by an English assassin, as the saviour of Wales, but they also saw possibilities in the figure of Roger Mortimer, descended from Llywelyn the Great. The poet Iolo Goch reminded him in 1385 that the blood of the red dragon ran in his veins. Mortimer may or may not have known the poem, but he would certainly have been familiar with the details of his princely ancestry and the dragon symbol.

During the 13th to the 16th centuries heraldry became ever more significant and popular, but in Wales no individual family ever bore a dragon on its coat of arms. Owain Glyndŵr had his own arms, derived from the princes of Powys, but when he proclaimed his rebellion in 1400 he did so under a red or golden dragon on white. On his privy seal of 1404 a dragon supports his coat of arms.

References in the 15th century, after the failure of both Owain Lawgoch and Glyndŵr, are more ambiguous. There's a splendidly optimistic line of 15th-century Welsh poetry which has become a proverb: *Y ddraig goch a ddyry gychwyn* – the red dragon gives the lead. Unfortunately for the dragon's dignity, the poet Deio ab Ieuan Du was using the red dragon metaphorically. His poem is a thank-you for the gift of a red bull, and in his enthusiasm for the bull's potency he describes the bull with a cow:

> They are like two dragons,
> To breed us calves and give milk;
> The red dragon [i.e. the bull] goes to it
> On the other's back beside the grove.

Hardly a patriotic symbol!

Despite the failure of Owain Glyndŵr's revolt, the dragon did not die. Jasper and Edmund Tudor used the dragon as crest and supporter on their arms in the Wars of the Roses, and Edmund's son Henry Tudor used a banner with a red dragon device on a green and white background on the battlefield at Bosworth in 1485, when he captured the crown from Richard III. The Great Chronicle of London tells that after his victory Henry went to St Paul's Cathedral to dedicate to God his 'red firye dragon beaten upon white and green sarsenet' along with other flags. Most remarkable of all, perhaps, is the splendid red dragon in the tracery lights above the Crucifixion in the great east window of King's College, Cambridge. For two generations the red dragon was used on the Tudors' royal coat of arms (apart from Mary I) as one of the two heraldic beasts supporting the shield; the other is an English lion. The shield itself quarters the fleur-de-lis of France with English lions. But why the green and white background? Let's postpone that until we discuss Welsh leeks.

The dragon's reign on the royal arms was short-lived; James I expelled the beast in favour of the unicorn from royal Scottish heraldry, and it retreated to Wales. It was briefly revived by Cromwell as the Protector's governmental arms, but in 1660 it disappeared from royal heraldry for two and a half centuries. Nevertheless the dragon survived on many legal seals, including three of the London courts and on documents of the Welsh Courts of Great Sessions.

During the 18th century, even as their culture was changing radically, the Welsh started to become more aware of the rich diversity of their past, and added to it some highly imaginative details. The most popular symbols of Welshness at that time were not the dragon, but the goat, the leek and the druid or bard, often with an associated harp or cromlech. All these appear in paintings and on a number of ballads, title pages and other devices, as will be seen in the next chapter. In the 19th century the dragon saw a revival in connection with the National Eisteddfod. By the century's last decades it was appearing frequently on Eisteddfod posters and carved into the magnificently uncomfortable chairs awarded annually to the champion poet.

Official interest in the dragon had revived a little in 1807, when a red dragon standing on a mound was pronounced the King's badge in Wales. In 1903 Edward VII assigned the badge to the new Prince of Wales. In 1910 a consortium of Welsh local authorities petitioned George V to include the red dragon on the Royal Standard and on coinage. The Privy Council decided this was 'not expedient', but as a concession the four lions of Gwynedd were included in the arms of the new Prince of Wales.

In 1953 a new royal badge of Wales was designed, with the dragon on its green and white ground surrounded with the motto *Y ddraig goch a ddyry gychwyn* and surmounted by a large crown. This was presented to Cabinet for approval. Prime Minister Winston Churchill was appalled. The Cabinet Secretary noted his grumpy comments:

> Odious design expressing nothing but spite, malice, ill-will and monstrosity. Words (Red Dragon takes the lead) are untrue and unduly flattering to [Aneurin] Bevan.

Churchill of course loathed Bevan, who had notoriously described Tories as 'lower than vermin'. His apparent belief that the College of Arms would want to flatter a turbulent socialist is quite bizarre. He didn't reply to Gwilym Lloyd-George's complaint that 'we get no recognition in Union, badge or flags'.

Despite Churchill's hostility, the new badge was adopted by the city of Cardiff as an extra ornament on its coat of arms, and for a while it appeared on a green and white flag for use on government buildings. Protests by the Gorsedd of Bards saw for the first time the red dragon on green and white taken up as the official flag of Wales. The badge does however live on as the stamp on statutory instruments made by the Welsh Assembly Government.

The dragon was to suffer another blow at official hands in 2008, when a new and more anodyne royal Welsh badge was adopted. Instead of the dragon, the lion shield of Gwynedd is surrounded by less provocative words from *Hen Wlad fy Nhadau*, 'Pleidiol wyf i'm gwlad', which translate rather feebly into English as 'I'm on the side of my country'. Even Churchill couldn't have objected. Interestingly, in view of recent anxiety about a possible break-up of the United Kingdom, the badge is surrounded by a wreath of the four national symbols: the rose, leek, shamrock and thistle in descending order each side.

Despite all these sideshows arranged by the College of Arms, the dragon has never made it back onto the royal coat of arms, although it would be perfectly possible, since the triple lions appear twice on the shield, quartered with the Irish harp and

Years after the world's national Post Offices had begun printing colourful regular stamps and frequent commemorative editions, the French and British systems remained conservative. Only the most unusual events were celebrated by special issues of British stamps – the Empire Exhibition of 1924, several royal occasions and the London Olympics of 1948. In 1955 a set of stamps celebrating British castles appeared, one of them showing Caernarfon. In 1958 Wales, Scotland and Northern Ireland were acknowledged with their own stamps at 3d., 6d. and 1s 6d. The Welsh stamps bore a large image of the Queen's head and a small dragon in the corner. But Welsh commemoratives were still sternly resisted. Two major events in Welsh history, the Patagonia settlement of 1865 and the Welsh New Testament of 1567 were rejected as beneath notice at the very time when Welsh cultural and political life were taking on new energy. However, the thaw continued. The range of symbols increased to include a leek designed to look like a Welsh love-spoon; the dragon grew in size, pushing the Queen's head into the corner. Daffodils and the Prince of Wales's feathers also appeared. In 1988 the anniversary of the Welsh Bible of 1588 was celebrated with four stamps which, thanks to their wide circulation, must have been the most widespread dissemination of the Welsh language in history. In 2009 the Post Office issued a set of stamps celebrating Wales. Welsh stamps and commemoratives are marginalised by the increasing use of franking machines, and by the sale of standard UK stamps in booklets. As in other spheres, one must ask to get what should be available automatically.

Scottish lion rampant. The Union Flag is another matter; the three crosses of George, Andrew and Patrick could hardly admit a dragon without looking a frightful mess. Neither could it easily accommodate the black-and-gold cross of St David, though this flag has become more used in recent years. An impasse remains.

The dragon enjoyed promotion to the Welsh one-pound decimal coinage in 1995, replacing the substantial leek which had occupied the coin's reverse side. But in 2005 the dragon was demoted, not without some protest on its behalf, in favour of the Menai suspension bridge, while bridges from Scotland, Ulster and northern English filled the reverse of other pound coins. Since then other Welsh one-pound designs have appeared.

So the dragon has survived for a millennium, not without vicissitudes, to represent Wales and Welshness. It has survived Norman conquest and Churchillian scorn; it has survived heraldic

Of all the dragon images visible today, the most flamboyant and most tragic is the extraordinary sculpture commemorating the World War I battle for Mametz Wood in July 1916, part of the enormous battle of the Somme. The wood lay on a ridge which the Allied High Command needed to capture. Royal Welsh Fusiliers' conscripts were sent into the teeth of German machine-gun fire, enduring at times misdirected British artillery, to achieve the objective at frightful cost. In his great poem 'In Parenthesis', David Jones wrote a harrowing yet strangely objective account of the battle, in which he, although a most unlikely soldier, took part. The slaughter and bloodshed was appalling. Robert Graves, an officer in the Welsh Fusiliers, wrote laconically:

Today I found in Mametz Wood
A certain cure for lust of blood.

cold-shouldering and gross commercial exploitation. The feeble effort of the National Front in Wales to produce a periodical under the dragon title has happily sunk without trace. Despite all the cuddly dragons in toyshops and children's books, the great beast can still be inspiring – especially when flying over the great Norman castles which were built to crush the Welsh. They're ours now. The Red Dragon is one of the most ancient flag-symbols in use anywhere, and it bids fair to last for centuries to come. There is life in the old monster yet.

Goats

Welsh goats? Why on earth? Why not Welsh cattle, Welsh sheep, Welsh pigs, Welsh ponies, Welsh dogs – all good domestic stock? The answer is that while there are Welsh breeds of all those farm animals, none is a national symbol of Wales as the goat has been – not even the Welsh Black or the Welsh Cob. That's why those Tories who hated Lloyd George used to pillory him as 'the Welsh Goat'; they loathed his Welshness as much as they detested his philandering.

Admittedly, as a Welsh icon the goat is not in the same league as the dragon or leek. I know of two Goat hotels, one of which is the Royal Goat at Beddgelert, but no Goat takeaways, laundries or rugby teams. It's not easy to discover why the goat has long been associated with Wales. But remember Shakespeare's peerless scene between Welsh Fluellyn and English Pistol in *Henry V*. The ridiculous Pistol's attempts to bait Fluellyn exasperate the Welshman so much that he determines to force the 'lousy scurvy knave' to endure humiliation. To which Pistol responds testily, 'Not for Cadwallader and all his goats', but he is compelled to submit nevertheless. Shakespeare knew well that the Tudors traced their royal Welsh ancestry to Cadwaladr the Blessed, revered as the last king of all the Britons, and he knew that goats were already linked with Wales.

Shakespeare's great contemporary Ben Jonson wrote a masque, *For the Honour of Wales,* in which the country's heroes are named: Llywelyn, Rhys ap Gruffudd, Cadwaladr, Caradog, and 'Owen Glendower with a Welsh hook and a goat-skin on his back' (a Welsh hook was an agricultural implement). Jonson's text, for all its dreadful rendering of Welsh accents and desire to get a laugh at any cost, is full of popular misinformation about Wales, as well as phrases in Welsh. But for all the friendly but patronising knockabout stuff, complete with a dance of Welsh goats, nevertheless the text finishes with perhaps the most fulsome praise of Wales ever written by an Englishman!

Nor was use of the goat confined to mockery of the Welsh in London. The late Francis Jones, examining Pembrokeshire court records for the year 1619, found a seal stamped with the royal coat of arms supported by a dragon and a goat. It would be good to find more examples. It is certainly clear that the goat was especially connected with Welshness, but why? Welsh hill-farmers kept goats into the 17th century, but they then disappear from farm inventories. English and Scottish hill-farmers certainly kept goats too. Nor is Wales alone in having flocks of feral goats in rugged territory; so do Devon, the Lake District and the wilds of Scotland. It isn't clear when domesticated goats, originally imported long before the Iron Age, succeeded in escaping and adapting to the mountain life; it might have happened soon after their actual arrival. Goats are slippery customers.

Throughout the 17th and 18th centuries the goat was certainly a major Welsh symbol. It usually served to mock the Welsh, and from the 1640s appears frequently in ballads, posters and chapbooks, as Peter Lord has shown. In *The Pleasant History of Taffy's Progress to London*, Taffy is shown on a goat's back. So do Shon-ap-Morgan and his wife Unaffred (i.e. Winifred) Shones in 1747, both also on their way to London. The great cartoonist James Gillray drew *A Welsh Tandem*, showing three Welshmen, with leeks in their hats, and three goats drawing their trap. As late at 1842 a print shows *The Political Drama in Honour of the Arrival of the Prince of Wales*, with each processional group led by goats. At their head is a man with a banner showing the Prince of Wales's feathers and the motto *Ich Dien* rendered as *Itch Dying*.

The reaction of the London Welsh to the goat jokes was to prefer the Prince of Wales's feathers as a proud patriotic symbol, though it derived from the medieval battlefields of Europe, not from Wales at all. It appears regularly as a statement of Welshness from the 1720s, became the crest of the Society of Cymmrodorion in 1751, and by the early 20th century had become the badge both of the Welsh Rugby Football Union and the Royal Welsh Fusiliers. It was an earlier generation of the Fusiliers who gave military and national dignity to the Welsh goat.

The Royal Welsh Fusiliers was one of the oldest regiments in the British army until demoted in 2005, when it became a battalion of the Royal Welsh Regiment but still kept the name. In 1777 the regiment's historian gave a colourful account of the ceremonies held by its officers on St David's Day, involving the regimental goat, cited below when we reach the subject of leeks.

In the way of the British army, the tradition held firm. In 1844 Queen Victoria was persuaded that a Billy goat from the royal flock should be presented to the regiment, and this sovereign's gift is an ongoing tradition in the Fusiliers' battalion. On St David's Day the goat is led around the mess table after dinner, led by the Goat Major (usually a lance-corporal), and escorted by a drummer, fifer and drum-major.

At this point I should warn readers that their faith in historical accuracy will be strained to the utmost by what now follows, but it is all documented, though not without a little confusion. The Fusiliers' goat is not a mascot, but a serving member of the unit, listed on the roll and ranked as a lance-corporal. The royal gifts of replacements as ageing goats retire have been provided from various sources, including allegedly the feral flock on the Great Orme, and are trained to behave themselves on parade. Goats have been taken on campaign; in 1873 the Fusiliers were sent to West Africa to subdue the Ashanti, and the goat unsurprisingly died in the oppressive climate, as did many of the soldiers. Another Fusilier goat was present in Berlin during the 1949 airlift.

These foreign travels cause quarantine problems, and each time the Fusiliers' goat returns to Britain an order has to be tabled in the House of Commons admitting him to the country without six months' delay in quarantine. When the Fusiliers moved at short notice from Jamaica to Bermuda for ceremonial duty at a summit meeting between Eisenhower and Churchill in 1952, the island authorities were reluctant to admit the animal, but Churchill ordered: 'Fumigate the goat and fly it in'. The Fusilier goat leads in all the battalion's ceremonial duties.

At a Queen's Birthday parade in 2006 in Cyprus, the Fusiliers' goat broke line and butted a drummer. He was put on a charge before the commanding officer and demoted from lance-corporal to Fusilier. However, a Canadian animal rights group heard of this and protested to the Ministry of Defence that the creature was only 'acting the goat' and should not be punished for behaving according to his nature. So he was brought back before the C.O. and his rank was restored.

The other Welsh unit with a ceremonial goat was the Welch Regiment, now also part of the Royal Welsh Regiment. Men of the Welch serving in the Crimean War were photographed with a goat, the first recorded for the unit, and from then on the regiment regularly maintained a goat, Taffy, performing similar duties to those of the Fusiliers' goats, especially on St David's Day. One goat, Taffy IV, served in France in 1914–15, retreated from Mons, was present at the first battle of Ypres and other conflicts before he died and was buried in Bethune. Although the goats of the regular army are tolerably well documented, there were certainly other Welsh military goats; several photos exist of a goat parading with the Cardiganshire Militia before World War I.

That is surely more than enough about Welsh goats, which still roam the Great Orme, Snowdonia and the hills of Llŷn, and are sometimes castigated for raiding the gardens of private houses. They are splendidly shaggy and horned, but not dangerous, and add a powerfully picturesque element to mountain views. But it is now time to turn to the more famous leek.

Leeks

The origin of the leek as a Welsh symbol is just as obscure as that of the goat. Shakespeare certainly knew about Welsh leeks. The humiliation of Pistol referred to above lies in his being forced to eat a raw leek, while King Henry is proud to claim that he wears a leek on St David's Day: 'for I am Welsh, good countryman,' claims the Monmouth-born monarch. The Welsh leek was established before Shakespeare's time; we know that Henry VIII, not known for his Welshness, paid 15 shillings (was it in jewel form?) for the gift to his daughter

Mary of a leek on St David's Day, so the custom was surely long established. Shakespeare's contemporary Michael Drayton, in his enormous poem *Poly-Olbion*, claims that St David ordered Welsh soldiers to wear leeks for mutual identification in battle against the English. I know of no earlier source for that particular legend, but it was enthusiastically taken up by a later versifier, Nehemiah Griffith, in his *The Leek. A Poem on St David's Day* (1717).

There is however a roundabout way of going further back. Whence came the green-and-white background for the red dragon flag? Not only is it claimed that Welsh soldiers at the Battle of Crécy in 1346 wore green and white, but the medieval Welsh poet Prydydd y Moch, writing before 1240, describes Llywelyn the Great leading 'a host of chieftains wearing green and white linen'. Did the Welsh adopt the leek because of its colours, OR were the colours chosen because they are the leek's colours? By 1485 – and presumably earlier – green and white had become the background for the Red Dragon.

The leek never lost its popularity. The 1777 description of the celebrations of St David's Day by the Royal Welsh Fusiliers tell us that:

> The Royal regiment of Welch Fuzileers has a privilegeous honor of passing in review preceded by a Goat with gilded horns, and adorned with ringlets of flowers… the corps values itself much on the ancientness of the custom.

The goat was led round the mess table three times, followed by a procession including a soldier bearing a silver salver of leeks and a loving-cup full of champagne. The youngest officer ate a raw leek to the accompaniment of a drum, then drank a champagne toast to St David. His example was then followed by all present who had not previously eaten the regimental leek. Non-commissioned officers and other ranks held similar ceremonies. As far as I can discover, all this has continued until the present day. Indeed, the leek has never lost its popularity, whether as a regimental badge, an ornament for rugby fans, or as an essential ingredient of *cawl* (Welsh lamb and vegetable stew).

Efforts to promote the daffodil as an alternative to the leek, or even as a replacement, cannot be traced further back than the end of the 19th century; I suspect Lloyd George was its originator – he was certainly a partisan. It was easily adopted, since in Welsh they bear similar names: *cennin* = leeks, *cennin Pedr* = daffodils. They can be persuaded in a good spring to flower for 1 March, and make a more convenient buttonhole that the leek. As such they have become popular, but the leek retains its symbolic and historic primacy.

Dragons, leeks and daffodils are only the most important of a string of Welsh icons, such as the harp, the black-hatted Welsh women's costume, the Welsh poppy now favoured by Plaid Cymru, and the Prince of Wales's feathers and motto. The motto, *Ich Dien* (I Serve) is not, as myth would have it, derived from Welsh *Eich Dyn* (Your Man). According to tradition, the plumes and motto were worn by blind King John of Bohemia, slain at the Battle of Crécy and thereafter adopted by Edward III's son the Black Prince, victor of the encounter. Other less romantic origins have been proposed, but a continental origin is certain.

2. Looking *for* The Welsh Border

Where does one country stop and another start? How can you tell? National borders are such strange creations. Some have been made by civil servants drawing lines on maps, often with the aid of a ruler. Some follow rivers, others follow mountain ranges. Some are invisible on the ground; others follow ditches, walls or even great ramparts of barbed wire or concrete. A few are hideously dangerous to approach. In their role as boundaries they are all man-made. There is no absolute need even for the sea to be a political boundary; think of the islands which compose Japan, New Zealand or Indonesia.

Unless we live on or close to a national border, it's only when we travel that borders impinge on our lives. Changes in Europe mean that many national frontiers seem to have vanished from sight. You only notice the transition from France to Belgium when bilingual signs start appearing on the roadside, or when you fail to buy a baguette in a Belgian village – the coinage is the same in both countries, it's the bread that's different. It seems to be very much the same on the Welsh-English border, where only the road-signs *Croeso i Gymru / Welcome to Wales*, and bilingual signs to *Trallwng / Welshpool* or *Aberhonddu / Brecon* tell the visitor that he's in another country. No fences, no walls, no gates, no controls – it's come and go as you please, unless you have to pay to cross one of the Severn bridges into Wales. Any route out of Wales is free.

There are of course suggestions of a natural frontier. When you approach Wales from Chester, from Shrewsbury, from Hereford or across the Severn Bridge, you can see the landscape slowly changing. You are moving from the English plains towards the Welsh hills. Of course there are hills in England not far from the Welsh border, but they seem rather individual and isolated compared with the larger bulk of the Black Mountains and Brecon Beacons in the south, the Cambrian range in mid Wales or the Berwyn and the Clwydian hills in the north. This is indeed different country, and largely because of those hills, this really is *a* different country.

There is nevertheless a fixed border, a national boundary between Wales and England, which has a long, complicated and rather odd history. The only historian to have written about it at any length is the anonymous contributor on the subject to wikipedia, and very useful his work is, even if he does insist on dating the parliamentary Act responsible for the border to the year 1535, while all other authorities prefer the correct modern dating of 1536.

Borders can exist in other, non-physical dimensions. There is the language border, discussed in the next chapter. There is a mental border, infinitely fascinating. It can be heard in jokes and the anti-Welsh put-downs still administered by English so-called comedians. It's there in the old Welsh proverb, *Calon y Sais wrth y Cymro*, difficult to translate. Roughly it implies that an Englishman's heart is ruthless and unforgiving in dealing with a Welshman. This mental border deserves a fuller treatment than anyone has yet given it.

How did these boundaries come to Wales? In the late fourth century AD the Roman government of southern Britain, besieged by enemies from west, north and east, began to buy off some of them by offering them the opportunity to settle within the island in order to help protect it. Germanic settlers from northern Europe moved to the east coast. As the Roman administration broke down during the early fifth century, these settlers started to spread westwards, followed by others. The nature of this process is so ill-documented that historians have argued about it for centuries. Did the British flee to the west (and to Brittany) to escape the ravening Anglo-Saxons? Were the British enslaved, even exterminated, in a process during which their language almost disappeared from the landscape? Or did they simply accept absorption by the incomers?

Whatever happened, it seems to have been more of a colonisation than a planned conquest, since these early English peoples had no central authority to direct them. From time to time there was certainly resistance by parts of the British population, and it took almost two hundred years for the settlers to reach the River Severn about 580 AD and the Irish Sea about 615 AD. Thus did the British peoples of Cumbria and the North, and those of the Devon-Cornwall peninsula, become separated from the Britons of the peninsula we call Wales?

This peninsula was so fragmented by its mountains and rivers that politically it fell naturally into small chiefdoms or minor kingdoms, which often fought each other. The Old English, themselves divided into smaller kingdoms for centuries, finally united under pressure from Norse-speaking settlers, who seriously threatened to turn England into a Scandinavian country. Meantime Welsh kingdoms shared a frontier with the powerful English kingdom of Mercia, and found themselves frequently under attack. The meaning of the name Mercia is simply 'Border People', so the Mercians were defining themselves in relation to the Welsh.

That Welsh-Mercian border was given physical expression in the eighth century by two great ditches and banks built by Mercian kings. The first, long known at Wat's Dyke, runs forty miles south from Basingwerk to Maesbury in Shropshire, and is attributed to King Aethelbald, who died in 757. The second, known for more than a thousand years as Offa's Dyke – Clawdd Offa in Welsh – was more ambitious. Offa, who died in 796, was the dominant figure in English history during his lifetime. The mighty Dyke is still disputed territory for archaeologists and historians. Asser, a Welshman writing in the tenth century, believed that the Dyke ran all the way from the coast of north Wales to the Severn estuary. The great scholar of the earthwork, Cyril Fox, agreed. His argument has recently been questioned, and it may be that the southern part of the Dyke, in which there are large gaps, was not an original part of such a sweeping concept. But Fox was surely right to see the course of the Dyke (at least in its northern two-thirds) as the result of local negotiations, leaving occasional communities of both peoples on the 'wrong' side. Fox demonstrated that on occasion the Dyke had to accommodate Welsh occupation of sites which Offa might well have preferred to have for himself.

The Dyke certainly did not keep Offa within any boundary; his troops invaded Wales in 778, 784 and again in 795. Clearly, although part of its purpose may have been defensive, the great Dyke was rather a starting point for the English than a buffer against the Welsh. Indeed, the popular version of English history used to tell us that the Dyke was to protect the poor helpless English, their wives and cattle, from the marauding and savage Welsh, but real history shows the opposite. Between the early eighth century and 1040 English armies invaded Wales at least 19 times! There was little military traffic the other way during that period.

Yet there is surely more to Offa's Dyke than its apparently aggressive/defensive purpose. What deeper motivation might underlie the concept of this majestic boundary bank – actually built by the sweated labour of the peasants who dwelt along its route? Offa perceived himself as a great king, a ruler who issued a significant coinage, a man of wealth and power. The other borders of Mercia, east, south and north, he stretched to include most of southern England, taking in peoples who spoke the same language and shared the same culture. He apparently felt no great need to impress them with dykes. But the Welsh were 'other', alien. *Anghyfiaith* is the Welsh word for the concept, meaning 'not of the same language or culture'. On the Welsh, politically divided as they were, Offa could and did make a great impression. So great indeed was that impression that the Welsh phrase, *Clawdd Offa*, is pregnant with meaning even to the present day. Going to England, for the Welsh, is still 'crossing Offa's Dyke'. The boundary is mental as well as physical.

For centuries the border fluctuated. Before Offa died the English had established a borough at Rhuddlan and occupied much of north-east Wales, from Oswestry to the River Clwyd, all administered as hundreds in the English mode. English settlers had moved westward into mid Wales; Radnor was a Saxon manor. Further south the largely Welsh population of Ewias and Archenfield remained within the Welsh diocese of distant St David's though coming under English rule.

By the eleventh century the kings of united England regarded themselves as overlords of a disunited Wales, though not as its rulers. When England fell to the Normans in 1066 it seemed, at least in retrospect, as if everything had changed – the Saxon royal family disappeared, its aristocracy had been wiped out near Hastings. Architecture, language, Church administration all changed. And yet nothing changed; the kingdom was still united, a much-altered language survived and triumphed, law and institutions were changed but not obliterated. The Normans conquerors were absorbed by those they had conquered.

Similarly, it might have seemed as if everything in Wales would change when the Normans crossed the Wye in 1067. Their onslaught was more vigorous and sustained than anything the English had previously mounted against the Welsh. They penetrated along the coasts and up the river valleys, building castles as they went. It was very different to their conquest of England, since there was no single king and army to oppose them; there was no single Welsh kingdom to conquer. Instead sovereignty in Wales was divided into cantrefs and commotes, which had to be taken piecemeal. Moreover it can be argued that very little changed, in that this was not occupation by the king of England. The actual boundary between English-occupied land and Welsh-inhabited land barely changed. The Norman barons were certainly subjects of the king, liable to give him service, but they did not extend his law or governance into Wales.

So there could be no single battle like Hastings to conquer such a tessellated country. The invaders made their gains commote by commote, cantref by cantref, creating lordships large and small as they went. Boundaries were everywhere, and they fluctuated. Even within a Norman lordship there would often develop an 'Englishry' and a 'Welshry'; in the latter the Welsh would be allowed to keep their own laws and customs, at least to a degree. Moreover the invaders intermarried with Welsh princesses and gave their own daughters to Welsh princes. Two Welsh princes even married royal princesses. The Normans heard Welsh legends through translators, eventually giving them currency throughout Europe as the tales of Arthur.

While Normans moved through Gwent into the Vale

of Glamorgan, Welsh lords clung to Caerleon and to the Glamorgan uplands. Normans drove up the Usk, Wye, Severn and Dee valleys; before 1100 there were Norman motte-and-bailey castles spread almost throughout the land. In particular they so subjugated the southern lands of Pembroke that there was a virtual ethnic cleansing, with settlers so replacing the native Welsh that almost all local place-names were lost for ever.

The Welsh found leaders who would fight back, preferring guerrilla and scorched earth methods of warfare, but learning how to build castles and how to storm them. The princes of Gwynedd regained the north-east as far as the Dee; Oswestry for a while became part of Powys. The lands governed by Norman incomers became known as the March; they were neither part of the realm of England nor subject to the king's law. Welsh princedoms and Marcher lordships fluctuated from decade to decade. Every map of Wales during this period looks like a jigsaw of boundaries.

After the death of Llywelyn the Last Prince in 1282 those boundaries became more or less fixed for two and a half centuries. In the Statute of Rhuddlan (1284) Edward I affirmed his conquest of Wales by dividing the country into March and Principality. The latter itself was divided into North (governed from Caernarfon) and South (governed from Carmarthen). The Marcher lordships themselves were a buffer zone between the Principality and the kingdom of England. The eastern boundary of the March did not exactly match the present-day line, which was established by the Laws in Wales Acts of 1536 and 1543 (until recently known as the Acts of Union). Nevertheless, that 13th-century boundary still looked remarkably like that of Offa. The apparently crazy ins and outs of the modern boundary certainly reflect medieval alterations, but the general outline of Wales in 750 and in 2012 is much the same.

The purpose of the Acts of 1536 and 1543 was to bring consistency of administration across England and Wales. From the viewpoint of London, where real power lay, the Marcher lordships and the Principality were anomalies, not at all conducive to good governance. This was at a time when Henry VIII and his chief minister, Thomas Cromwell – both men of Welsh paternity – saw the need for uniform administration in the face of foreign threats following the separation from Rome. So Wales was to be united with England as a single legal realm. This meant the abolition of the Marcher lordships and their embodiment, along with the Principality, as counties, with justices of the peace and members of parliament, all after the English model.

> Owain Glyndŵr certainly tried to revolutionise the border between Wales and England. At the height of his rebellion in 1404–07 he conspired against Henry IV with English rebels. His hope was to achieve a Greater Wales reaching as far as Worcester, but the rebels were defeated. Owain's other dreams of independence for a principality with its own government, Church and universities have to some extent become fact. But the vision of an extended Wales died with him.

Making the new county boundaries involved allotting the Marcher lordships to counties. There was still an anomaly at the northern end, where Maelor Saesneg was left as a separate part of Flintshire, along with a little enclave of Flintshire near Holt, isolated in the new county of Denbighshire. The lordships of Oswestry, Caus, Bishop's Castle and Clun became part of Shropshire, while Huntington, Clifford and Ewyas Lacy were apportioned to Herefordshire. The other lordships, all the way from Hawarden and Mold to Chepstow and along the south coast to Pembroke, formed parts of new Welsh counties.

The line drawn up in 1536 between the English and Welsh counties remains unchanged to the present day, having been confirmed by the Local Government Act of 1972. It looks extraordinarily erratic. Within a few miles of its starting point on the Dee estuary it runs sometimes south-east, sometimes south-west. Rarely indeed does it run so directly north-south as does Offa's Dyke. It follows rivers: the Dee, Vyrnwy, Teme, Monnow and finally the Wye, whose gorge is the most natural formation on the whole border. Once the border reaches the Severn it extends into the estuary to include the island of Flat Holm, while Steep Holm is in England.

When drawn up the border did not entirely respect the boundaries of the two existing eastern dioceses of Llandaff and St Asaph. Several parishes in Wales still belong to Hereford and Chester dioceses. Nor did the border respect the language boundary; several Welsh-speaking communities were included in Shropshire and Herefordshire. It even divided the little town of Saltney by running down the inevitably named Boundary Lane. The village of Llanymynech, too, was divided by its main street. Such apparent anomalies were of no concern to Henry's legal draftsmen, since they were incorporating Wales *into* England.

The Act of 1536 sorted out one early boundary anomaly. One of the oddities of the line of Offa's Dyke is its southernmost end. It reaches the Severn estuary a mile east of the river Wye, which suggests that that little strip of land apparently counted as Welsh whenever that part of the Dyke was built. But in any case there had been some kind of Welsh 'creep' eastwards. The parishes of Tidenham and Woolaston, whose churches lay east of the Wye, were firmly included in Gloucestershire by the Act of 1536.

The biggest anomaly of all was the new county of Monmouthshire. The Acts of 1536 and 1543 had created 13 counties. Wales was to be subject to England law, but its administration was to be different. For the sake of that neatness typical of a certain kind of legal mentality, four new circuits of Great Sessions of Wales would be created, each with three counties. Monmouth was left over, and therefore incorporated into the Oxford legal circuit. Hence the division of opinion – is Monmouthshire in Wales or England? From most practical points of view it hardly mattered, since English legislation was made with all Wales in mind. Monmouth remained within the Welsh diocese of Llandaff, but since all the Welsh dioceses were part of the Church of England that hardly mattered either. Sentiment was and is a different matter, well expressed by Shakespeare in *Henry V*, written of course sixty years after the Acts on Laws in Wales, where he twice makes the young king affirm that he is Welsh, thanks to his birth in Monmouth.

Of the other border anomalies, Maelor Saesneg is particularly intriguing. Once the home of the great monastery of Bangor-on-Dee, in the eighth century it was firmly part of Mercia. By 1086 it belonged to Cheshire. However, about 1201 Madog ap Gruffudd of Powys seems to have been able to take it over, and it became part of northern Powys. However, when Madog's son Gruffydd died in 1269 it became the dower land of his English widow, Emma Audley. In 1278 she resigned it to the Crown, and in 1284 Edward I decreed it to be a detached part of Flintshire, so it became Welsh again. Centuries later the Boundaries Commission of 1887 discussed the status of Maelor Saesneg. A public meeting at Overton and a meeting of the Flintshire justices of the peace both favoured moving it to Shropshire, but nothing was done to change the status of this, the most English part of Wales.

From 1543, then, the Welsh-English border had virtually no political significance. Wales was administered by the Council for Wales and the Marches from its base at Ludlow until 1689, when it was abolished. It had been intended to advise the Princes of Wales in governing the whole area of Wales along with Cheshire, Shropshire, Worcestershire, and Herefordshire – very much the area that Glyndŵr had dreamed of ruling. Often there would be no Prince of Wales (as from 1553 till 1603, for example), but the Council had a President. The Council was much resented by the English counties, and in fact it functioned mainly as a court of law until its abolition, leaving the title of Prince of Wales devoid of political or administrative significance.

Wales as a political concept vanished entirely when an Act of 1746 laid down 'that where the Kingdom of England... hath been or shall be mentioned in any Act of Parliament, the same has been and shall... be deemed and taken to comprehend and include the Dominion of Wales'. A final kick was delivered by an Act of 1830 to abolish the Courts of Great Sessions in Wales, the only legal or administrative difference between the two countries. Wales was now a geographical area, without political or legal identity, nor any national institutions until 1811.

There was however still a boundary between Wales and England. It existed in several forms. Travellers to Wales frequently commented on the poverty of Wales as they passed into the country. They noticed the Welsh language, whether they called it the gibberish of Taffydom or, as did Dr Samuel Johnson, express appreciation and concern for the language. After all, it was still the language of the great majority of Welsh people.

Socio-cultural boundaries between England and Wales did of course tend to shift in favour of English culture. The gentry became first bilingual, then largely Anglophone. Personal names had moved to the English system of inherited patronymics, though it took a long time for the rural population, especially in the west, first to drop the *ap/ach* formation (Dafydd ap Gwilym = David son of William > David Williams, Marged ach Ifan = Margaret daughter of Evan > Margaret Evans), then to adopt the inherited patronymic rather than one's own father's particular name. Married women started using their husband's surnames later than in England. Welsh styles of dress and forms of entertainment tended towards English models.

But other changes happened too. There had been no religious barriers in Wales such as had come into existence in Ireland and in the Scottish islands. The Welsh had expressed little resistance to the Protestant Reformation, but from 1740 onwards Wales moved slowly but firmly away from loyalty to the Anglican Church. Methodists within the Church, mostly of Calvinist persuasion, broke away in 1811 to become the Calvinistic Methodist Church of Wales (now the Presbyterian Church of Wales). Even though farmers still had to pay tithes for the support of the Church of England, they became increasingly loyal either to Calvinistic Methodism or to their Baptist or Congregational churches. By the mid 19th century Wales was essentially Nonconformist. This helped a growing awareness of national differences. From the late 18th century Welsh history, Welsh landscape (and therefore Welsh art), Welsh literature and Welsh music had become of increasing interest to an increasing intelligentsia. By the end of the 19th century a new cultural difference had emerged with the growth of competitive games. Wales became a separate country in terms of international football, rugby and many other sports, though not cricket (see chapter 11).

Politically, the rapid collapse from 1860 of the landowners' monopoly of Welsh parliamentary seats, the increasing franchise, a growing moral awareness and national self-consciousness meant that political change was bound to come about. The Act of 1881 against Sunday opening of public houses in Wales was the first piece of Wales-only legislation to issue from Westminster for centuries (Monmouthshire was included in 1921). The Wales-England boundary once more had legal meaning. That was followed by the Welsh Education Act of 1889 and the establishment in 1907 of the Central Welsh Board of Education, now the Welsh Joint Education Committee, though it had no responsibility for the nascent University College of Wales (note the title) established at Aberystwyth in 1872. Another step was the disestablishment in 1920 of the four Welsh dioceses, which became the Church in Wales. Even if the new ecclesiastical boundary was not entirely identical with the political boundary, it was another affirmation of national difference. All these changes strengthened the mental boundary even as industry and transport linked Wales ever closer to her neighbour.

There were other signs of devolution. In 1908 the Royal Commission on Ancient and Historical Monuments in Wales and Monmouthshire was established. The Welsh Board of Health was created in 1919, and the Welsh Department of the Ministry of Agriculture and Fisheries in 1922. All these moves affirmed the increasing importance of the national border. It was still highly porous; children crossed the border to go to the nearest school, sick people in Wales near English hospitals were taken as patients.

There was then a hiatus in this process of devolution, but it recommenced after World War II. Churchill's 1951 government appointed a part-time minister for Wales, a role filled by the

Home Secretary David Maxwell-Fyfe, known as Dai Bananas. A more significant appointment was that of a Secretary of State for Wales in 1964 and the Welsh Office in 1965, with many new responsibilities. When the Welsh counties were reorganised in 1974 and again in 1996, with drastic alteration of their boundaries, the national border remained untouched.

Since the establishment of the Welsh Assembly Government in 1999 the border matters more than it has for many centuries. Differing national policies and expenditure on health, education, agriculture and public transport affect people who may be living only a few hundred yards apart. Since not one of the border constituencies had voted in favour of devolution in the 1997 referendum, it is noteworthy that they have accepted their new status in a devolved Wales with remarkably little fuss. There is even a 2006 website inviting the people of Herefordshire to vote to join Wales, on the grounds that the Welsh Assembly government's agricultural administration is much more efficient than London's. However, the prospect of an additional Welsh county is extremely unlikely. On 3 March 2011 the border was strengthened by a referendum giving the Welsh Assembly limited powers to legislate – in other words, to beef up the Assembly at a time when Wales was due to lose a quarter of its MPs. This time 21 of the 22 authorities registered positive votes; only Monmouthshire voted 'No' by a tiny majority.

The boundary has certainly been strengthened since devolution in matters of legal administration. There is now a Court of Appeal in Cardiff to hear challenges to decisions taken by the Assembly Government. Until 2007 Wales with Chester was one of the six administrative units of the court system in England and Wales. Now Wales stands as a unit by itself for purposes of administering the Magistrates, County and Crown courts of Wales, as well as the police and probation services. Talk of a single Police Service for Wales is heard. Senior lawyers in Wales and London are actively discussing the possibilities of juridical changes which may strengthen the national boundary still further. Meanwhile, Saltney and Llanymynech both remain divided by the boundary of 1536, which meant so little at the time, and now means so much more.

3. Looking *for* The Welsh Language

Silly title! The Welsh language is to be seen almost everywhere in Wales. The signposts smack you between the eyes when you cross the border. *Croeso i Gymru* is the first, swiftly followed by directional signs to Newport / Casnewydd, to Brecon / Aberhonddu, to Welshpool / Trallwng, to Mold / Yr Wyddgrug. It doesn't take long to realise that each sign points to one place. Sometimes you may wonder why anyone bothers with a sign like Wrexham / Wrecsam, but when the Great Sign Change came about several decades ago the nervous authorities didn't want to be accused of shoving Welsh down people's throats. We'll return to the subject of the Great Sign Change later.

What must strike a curious visitor is that there are so many places with two distinct names. Travel down the Welsh border and there are Chirk / Y Waun, Presteigne / Llanandras, Chepstow / Cas-gwent. These immediately remind us that the English language has long been represented in Wales. In those three examples both the Welsh and English names are long-established, and have totally different meanings. Other pairs of names show that one is a version of the other: Newtown / Trenewydd, Cardiff / Caerdydd.

The long, long encounter of Welsh and English is well exemplified in place-names, not only in Wales but in England too. The vast majority of English names derive either from Old English or Norse, but as English settlers moved slowly westwards they adopted some place-names from the British language – Kent, Dover, London, Leatherhead, York – and more, especially river-names: Thames, Trent, Derwent,

Severn, Avon, Exe. Sometimes, confronted by landmarks, they took the local British word and added their own version, so there are village names like Chetwood (*chet* from Welsh *coed* meaning 'wood') and Churchill (Welsh *crug* = mound + English *hill*) – nothing to do with a church, though if you find that hard to believe, scholars will tell you that it is indeed so.

The western peninsulas of Wales and Cornwall were less easily taken over than the eastern lands, and there Welsh (and for centuries Cornish) remained dominant. However the warriors of Mercia, the great kingdom of middle England, pressed frequently into Wales. They even christened Wales's highest mountain with an early English name, Snawdune; it could after all be seen from a long way off. As for Anglesey, on the other hand, although that *Angle-* sounds English, the name is a Viking one – the island of Ongul, though we have no idea who Ongul was. There are many Viking names round the Welsh coast.

It was really the assault begun by the Normans that saw the doubling-up of place-names in Wales. Sometimes they founded a settlement and gave a name of their own – Newport, for example – while the Welsh quickly produced their own name, Casnewydd (a rough translation). Sometimes the Normans heard Welsh names which made no sense to them, so they garbled the Welsh even beyond recognition, as when Ynysgynwraidd became Skenfrith and Ystumllwynarth became Oystermouth. This may look unlikely, but it's true! Indeed, it's still going on; when visitors to Wales see a name like Rhyd-y-pennau it's easy to anglicise it as *Ride-a-penny*, to the despair of locals. When writing became common and when maps were made, anglicised spellings of Welsh were usual, so for centuries Llanelly and Carnarvon were the usual spellings for those names – until the Great Sign Change.

In the meantime a one-sided process of borrowing words as well as names began, over a thousand years ago. By today thousands of terms have been borrowed from English into Welsh. But before we look at this process, we must ask – why didn't it work both ways? Only a handful of Welsh words have been borrowed into English – hog, brat, flannel, eisteddfod, cwm. This is particularly striking when compared, for example, with the number of Native American words borrowed into English: tomahawk, tipi, wigwam, powwow, pemmican, papoose, squaw, moccasin, skunk, moose, pecan, toboggan, tobacco are only some of the many.

Why this difference? Why so few Welsh loan-words in English? It is best explained simply by the fact that the material culture of the Anglo-Saxon settlers differed little from that of the people whose land they colonised – both peoples depended on farming. The settlers had their own words for almost everything they came across in western Britain, so they didn't need new words. English settlers in North America, on the other hand, found trees, crops, animals and numerous inventions for which they had no words – so they borrowed the native terms. English has never been ashamed to borrow words, but it can really bother learners of Welsh that they hear the spoken language sprinkled with English terms – a problem not confined to Wales, as members of the French Academy would testify.

Indeed it's part of the genius of the English language that loanwords are quickly at home on the tongue. Hitler promised lighting war, and *blitzkrieg* immediately entered English, soon modified to *blitz*. The Soviets launched the first orbiting space satellite, and *sputnik* was immediately picked up. So supple is the structure of English, so diverse its vocabulary – it consists largely of borrowed words – that new terms sit comfortably within it. Welsh finds it less easy, but borrows just the same. In Iceland, by contrast, foreign words are rigorously avoided and newly-coined Icelandic terms used instead.

Yet if the material culture of Anglo-Saxon England was not seriously different from that of the British who became Welsh, why did words move westwards rather than eastwards? After all, the Welsh began borrowing words from Old English more than a thousand years ago – *hosan, capan, sidan, ffordd, bwrdd* are just a handful. Fraternisation began early, as the word *cusan* (a kiss) demonstrates – there was love as well as hatred between the two peoples. The whole subject is obviously a matter of power relationships. It may have taken the Saxon settlers two centuries to reach what is now the Welsh border from the beaches of eastern England; they were colonists rather than conquerors. But they were dynamic; they were organised, they were on the move, they were dominant. This had its profound effects on the psychology of the Welsh. That is a complex subject indeed, perhaps best crystallised as follows.

Gruffydd Robert was a Welsh Catholic scholar who published a remarkable Welsh grammar when living in Milan in exile in 1567. The book is in the form of a dialogue. One character laments that a Welshman travelling to England no sooner hears Shrewsbury's bells than he forgets his Welsh and speaks only bad English. Not all Welsh people have done that, of course, but it is typical of the phenomenon known as internal colonisation. The Welsh traveller knows, without having to think about it, that England is much larger, more populous and wealthier than his own country. He feels that he must gain acceptance, and that can only be won by learning English, since he knows that no-one in England is likely to speak Welsh to him. There are of course degrees of acceptance – Gruffydd Robert's traveller believed that not only the use of English (natural enough) but denial of his own culture was necessary to make progress in his new surroundings. He was not, and is still not alone in this belief. It's seen as part of 'getting on in the world' – in a word, Progress, that great psychological enemy of minority languages.

The whole development of Welsh was further complicated by one long process and by one sudden event. The long process was the use of Latin. From the first writings by Welshmen in the fifth century AD until its gradual decline from the 16th century onward, Latin was the true language of prestige throughout western Christian Europe – the language of the Church, the language of government and law, the premier language of culture. All European languages borrowed from Latin, if indeed they weren't already its offspring. The first published Welsh grammar was written in Latin in 1621. The first major Welsh dictionary was a Latin-Welsh/Welsh-Latin dictionary in 1632.

The sudden event was the Norman conquest of England with its long-term consequences for Wales. Overnight French, not English, was the language of prestige, of court and culture. Old English, a language of high culture and legal usage, suddenly became the tongue of peasants. But ten thousand Norman settlers found themselves ruling well over a million speakers of a very different language. Old English was suddenly downgraded to largely oral usage. During the next generations spoken English changed so dramatically that had there been sufficient Norman invaders and settlers of both sexes, English might have withered into a series of local peasant dialects. But despite the brief supremacy of French-speaking culture, English survived and triumphed by sheer weight of numbers.

Of course Wales too was affected by Norman French; it gained a few place-names and a number of loan-words, but it was nothing like the impact of French on English. In a remarkable example of counter-colonisation, the Normans somehow picked up enough knowledge of Welsh culture to adopt and adapt Welsh history and legend to their own ends. The court of an Anglo-Norman baron would hear English, French and Welsh spoken and Latin used in church and administration. The court of a Welsh prince might experience all that, plus the possible shock of intermarriage with the incomers, as when in 1205 Llywelyn ap Iorwerth ('the Great') married 14-year-old Joan (Siwan), daughter of King John. She brought with her a large retinue of servants both francophone and anglophone, but without a word of Welsh between them. What language did Llywelyn and Joan use in bed and at board?

More importantly for Welsh, now opened to wider European culture, there was a huge invigoration of the native language by what is called for convenience the twelfth-century Renaissance. Welsh stories, poems, laws, history, religious material and medical lore were all written down, and much Latin material was translated into Welsh. Such cultural capital was to be of the greatest importance to the morale of the nation for centuries to come. This was especially the case because it meant there was a standard literary and legal language understood right across Wales. In Brittany there was no similar bulk of native written culture to give uniformity to the Breton language, which survived by weight of numbers but in very different dialects.

Welsh was particularly fortunate in that the Edwardian conquest and settlement of 1284 did not cause the total subjection of the people under external rule. Despite the Marcher lords, despite imposed Crown officials, a ruling class eventually emerged largely from among free Welsh landowners. They inherited much of the earlier princely culture, especially its custom of patronising poets who travelled from place to place singing the praises of those who paid them. This was not a mere exercise in toadyism. It gave valued status to the poets themselves as well as confirming the prestige of the landowners, who were reminded of the values of their culture, one of which was *amlder Cymraeg* – a wealth or richness of Welsh.

It could not last – in the world of spoken language, nothing does. With the 16th-century legal unification of Wales and England, with the latter reaching one of the high points of her history, the Welsh gentry turned more and more to education in Oxford and the Inns of Court. They gained access to the House of Commons. They moved to the English surname system, not by compulsion but by the desire for identification in the English mode. Anglo-Welsh marriages became ever commoner, English penetrated Welsh culture ever more deeply. The poets no longer had the same welcome; the traditional round of praise was abandoned.

Yet the very period which saw this tectonic shift in attitudes was countered by the linguistic ideals of the Reformation. True, Wales was to be united even more firmly with England under the brand-new English Church with its espousal of worship and reading in the vernacular. But Wales had its own vernacular, cherished by a number of outstanding humanist scholars. Clearly it was wiser to allow the Welsh to read the Scriptures and the new Book of Common Prayer in the language of the people, rather than leave them in religious darkness. In 1567 the New Testament and Book of Common Prayer were published in Welsh, by Act of Parliament, so that the Reformation (in its peculiar English version) could take root in Wales. A Catholic Wales could have been a seed-bed for the kind of rebellion which actually happened in Cornwall. After the hesitant start of 1567, the man was at hand who could make it really happen – William Morgan. He took the rich vocabulary, the *amlder Cymraeg* of the poets, and turned it to serve a new, powerful prose style into which he translated the Old Testament and revised the New, published in 1588 with the royal coat of arms, supported by the Tudor red dragon, on the title page. Every Sunday the population could and did hear the word of God in their own language, the same language across Wales. Of the six living Celtic languages (Irish, Scots Gaelic, Breton, Cornish, Manx and Welsh) only Welsh gained that status.

So Welsh alone began slowly to enjoy the advantages of the printing press. The first surviving Welsh-language book had been published in London in 1546. Apart from the prestigious religious texts referred to above, progress was sluggish. But through the 17th century a small but steady number of Welsh texts were printed. By the 18th century, with the beginnings of popular education, numbers increased and prices decreased, making at least almanacs, ballads and pamphlets available to all except paupers. The great majority of books were religious, encouraged by the growth of devout nonconformity.

London has always had primacy among printers in England; indeed, until 1694 printing was confined to London and the universities of Oxford and Cambridge. But then presses soon appeared in Shrewsbury and spread via Newcastle Emlyn (Adpar, 1718) to Carmarthen in 1722 and thence across Wales, supplemented by presses in Bristol, Chester, Dublin and still-active Shrewsbury. By 1850 every town, however small, except in Radnorshire, east Monmouthshire and south Pembrokeshire, had a printing press producing material in Welsh and often in English too. Periodicals and weekly newspapers only really began to develop, slowly at first, in the 19th century, but in the heyday of the Welsh weekly newspaper after the repeal of the Stamp Act in 1855, a number of successful titles flourished in both north and south Wales, most notably Thomas Gee's influential *Baner ac Amserau Cymru* from 1859.

The spread of literacy and cheaper publishing, with ease of carriage thanks to the spreading railway network, brought about a golden age of Welsh publishing from 1855 to 1890. Huge numbers of books, pamphlets, almanacs and ballads were sold throughout Wales. However, the writing on the wall was in English. It prophesied the imminent death of the Welsh language and the identification of the English language with Progress. The commissioners for education in Wales reported in 1847 that thanks to his language, '[the Welshman] is left to live in an under-world of his own, and the march of society goes so completely over his head that he is never heard of.' In 1867 *The Times* thundered that 'the Welsh language is the curse of Wales... The sooner all Welsh specialists disappear from the face of the Earth, the better.' The arrogance of the imperialist monoglot was never better expressed.

At the very same time the number of Welsh-speakers was increasing and consuming the growing number of Welsh publications. Nevertheless, pressure on the language, already centuries old, was getting worse, especially with the establishment of compulsory education from 1870. For two generations Welsh barely figured in the schools of Wales. Vigorous industrialisation in the south-east and north-east, once fuelled by Welsh-speaking workers from farms and fields, was by 1900 drawing large numbers of immigrants from England and beyond. The linguistic border between dominant English and dominant

Welsh began to move westwards. Although the number of Welsh-speakers continued to increase until 1911, the percentage of Welsh-speakers was diminishing. Inevitably there was ever more marriage between Welsh- and English-speakers.

Government and local government involvement in the lives of individuals increased rapidly – and administration was in English. English, too, was the language of justice, the main language of public life. Only in the religious and cultural sphere could Welsh raise its voice, but even the National Eisteddfod was staged largely in English. The early 20th century dealt a series of thunderbolt shocks to Welsh. The Great War drilled scores of thousands of men in English, and killed tens of thousands. Then economic decline began, accelerating into the 1930s with mass emigration to England. By contrast there was an extraordinary revival of literature and scholarship in Welsh. That this was at least partly due to increased education is suggested by the parallel development of literature in English by Welsh writers. Meantime the decline of the Welsh-speaking population continued through 1921, 1931 and 1951, after another war had brought evacuees, compulsory recruitment for both Forces and labour, inevitably driving the language further into retreat.

However, once the whole country had begun seriously to recover after World War II, a new vigour in cultural life gradually appeared. The only really serious effort on behalf of the Welsh language in the 1920s had been the founding of *Urdd Gobaith Cymru*, the Welsh League of Youth, still vigorous ninety years later, and the more hesitant establishment of Plaid Cymru. But from 1939 interest began to grow in the idea of separate schools where Welsh would be the main language of life and learning. After a hesitant start, this movement gained the support of local and national government. Today

Welsh-language teaching is available to the children of parents who make that choice almost throughout Wales.

Much of the inspiration for political and linguistic activity in Welsh terms can be seen to have derived from an apparently isolated event in 1936. A remarkable protest by three prominent men in Welsh cultural life, all members of Plaid Genedlaethol Cymru, the Welsh National Party, who staged a fire at the site of a government-imposed bombing school on the Llŷn peninsula, gave themselves up and were jailed. The excitement fizzled out, but was revived early in the 1960s when one of the three, Saunders Lewis, gave an impassioned lecture on the BBC on St David's Day 1962, *Tynged yr Iaith*, the Fate of the Language.

Lewis called for sacrificial direct action to secure legal status for the Welsh language. Young people, especially students at the colleges of the University of Wales, responded by painting out official English-language signs and sitting down in government premises, demanding that government literature and signs be in Welsh as well as English. The protestors formed Cymdeithas yr Iaith Gymraeg, the Welsh Language Society, to coordinate and support their efforts. Hundreds, including the inspirational balladeer Dafydd Iwan, went to jail rather than pay the fines imposed on them for their actions. Inevitably the appeal fell at first on deaf ears, but when university professors and ministers of religion, along with other senior members of society, began to protest too, usually in a more 'respectable' manner than the younger generation, then change was inevitable. Acts of Parliament were passed, the first a milk-and-water affair in 1967, followed at intervals by more legislation, until by now the legal status of Welsh is secure.

This was the time of the Great Sign Change, when Llanelly became Llanelli, when Carnarvon became Caernarfon, and when a host of paired bilingual names appeared on signs. So Denbigh added Dinbych to its signs, Mold added Yr Wyddgrug, Carmarthen was joined by Caerfyrddin and Abertawe linked to Swansea. The historic counties once again displayed their names proudly, only to be largely hidden during the revision of local government of the 1970s. The planners of that change were able to restore even more historic names across the country: Dyfed from the *Mabinogion* for the south-west, the principalities of Powys and Gwynedd in the north and east, Clwyd, Morgannwg and Gwent elsewhere. The reform of the 1990s saw them changed again; Powys and a diminished Gwynedd remained, Dyfed and Gwent vanished, while Morgannwg (Glamorgan) was vastly reduced to the Vale of Glamorgan / Bro Morgannwg.

Other developments ran alongside these changes. One was the growth of Welsh-language broadcasting, bringing all-day radio services in Welsh and English. Welsh-language television was much more controversial, but once a new generation of protestors had grappled with the issue, change was inevitable. Finally, after Gwynfor Evans threatened to fast to death, the government gave way and a Welsh-language television channel, S4C, was established; it began broadcasting in 1982. Another development was a change of heart in the world of commerce. Banks and an increasing number of supermarket chains began to make public gestures towards the language, printing forms in Welsh or bilingually and putting up bilingual signs. The hostility which was once expressed, especially in parts of the south-east, towards the use of Welsh has largely evaporated. Visits to Newport and Ebbw Vale by the National Eisteddfod in recent decades brought in huge numbers of sympathetic local visitors as well as the devotees who go every year.

A third development has been the appearance of many activities devoted in one way or another to the use of Welsh. A Welsh-language women's movement, Merched y Wawr, was founded, as were Welsh dining clubs and societies involved in history and the countryside. Offset-litho printing made it possible to publish local monthly papers, *papurau bro,* right across Wales, sustained by voluntary work. Bookshops dedicated to selling Welsh books and other materials spread across the country. A Welsh-language pop and rock music scene grew slowly from the 1960s onwards, supported by a recording industry.

Indeed, this burgeoning of activity had economic significance. A major stick with which to beat the Welsh language had been its supposed economic insignificance. But by the 1980s there were bookshops, publishers, television, theatre and recording companies all devoted to working through Welsh, giving employment to Welsh-speakers. A knowledge of Welsh was never more useful than today.

However, it should not be supposed that all is well. From the 1960s onwards there was an increasing movement of people from beyond Wales into the Welsh rural heartland, where hitherto the language of most primary school playgrounds had been overwhelmingly Welsh. It was not only retired people, but economic migrants who sought to live and bring up families in Wales. Some were sympathetic to the language, others less so. Schools which as late as 1940 had been able to teach Welsh to hundreds of evacuees now found themselves being linguistically overwhelmed. Rising house prices made it difficult for many Welsh families to remain in their communities.

At the same time there could be little doubt that the same kind of linguistic change that was happening to English was affecting Welsh to an even greater extent. A less rigorous attitude to standards of linguistic purity, common today in many cultures, was having its effect on Welsh. It was not simply a matter of English loan-words. English idioms have been busy colonising Welsh. English colloquialisms are often literally translated, at the level of *tro'r golau ar* (switch the light on), *rhowch ffordd* (give way) which grate horribly on a traditional speaker's ear. This is more than a matter of inevitable linguistic change. If a language is to flourish, it needs its own integrity of structure, its own idioms. Welsh suffers by the loss of the influence of the Bible and the pulpit, somewhat as English does by the failure of modern-language learning in schools and from its own commercial dominance.

The richness of Welsh vocabulary has changed, not only through the adoption of English words but from the disappearance of traditional ways of life and their terminology. The lack of a range of powerful media to compare with English-language television, radio and newspapers makes it difficult for new Welsh words to be adopted quickly; it's easier to incorporate English terms which have become known to everyone overnight. The BBC does its best to compensate in the circumstances.

There is now much encouragement for adults to learn Welsh; a network of classes covers almost the whole country. But the drop-out rate is high. It is almost impossible for people living an English-speaking life to learn a new language in one or two classes a week. Much better, for those able to take advantage of them, are the Wlpan semi-immersion courses held in several centres. The name was borrowed from the successful movement in Israel to teach Hebrew to immigrants. Welsh may be easier to learn than Hebrew, and it has the advantage of a near-phonetic orthography, making it easy to read. But it does have complications which can mystify a newcomer, especially anyone who knows only one language and especially as that one language is usually English.

English is rather special among the languages of Europe. It has virtually abolished the gender of nouns, so for example instead of *le/la* in French there is only one word, *the*. There's no need to worry about making the adjective agree with its noun, as there is in French. *He/she* in English are only used of people and of animals of defined gender; otherwise English uses the unique word *it*. No need to worry whether a book is masculine or feminine. Moreover the verb in English has only four forms: *love, loves, loved* and *loving*. But English makes up for all that simplicity by using a host of complex auxiliaries: *shall, will, was, were, is, are, do, did, has, have, had, should, would, may, might, could,* not to mention expressions such as *might have been*. Then of course there's the colossal vocabulary and the eccentricities of English spelling: *bough, rough, cough, though, through, thorough, lough…*

The complications of Welsh include the basic matter of saying 'yes' and 'no'. You can grasp this by trying to answer questions in English without using those two simple words. For example, 'Will you come to town tonight?' can be answered 'I will' or 'I won't'. So in Welsh speech the listener's answer is determined by the form of the question. Then there's the numerous ways of forming plurals. Welsh has another surprising element – the 'conjugated preposition', in which prepositions and pronouns are linked together as single words, like *amdanaf* = 'about me'. Most notorious is the system of lenitions or mutations. Thus the initial letter of a word may need to be changed according to its relationship to words around it. This applies to words beginning with *p, c, t b, g, d, m, rh* and *ll*. So learner-readers of Welsh will find in their texts words which don't appear in their dictionaries. One really needs a stout heart to win through.

Why bother? All Welsh people speak English! To which, as one lucky enough to have experienced learning by immersion, I would give several answers. To be without Welsh in Wales is a kind of deafness. The land speaks to you through its place-names, it speaks through its literature and culture, it speaks to you on the tongues of those for whom it is their first language. This is not unique to Wales – every traveller in other countries knows it. Each language is for its speakers both a mirror reflecting themselves back, and a window giving its own view of the world. The potential loss of any language is a tragedy, one that is being repeated frequently across the world. Numerically speaking, Welsh is among the top 15 per cent of the world's 6,000 languages. But given its circumstances, Welsh is on the cusp between vigorous survival and becoming moribund. It contains within itself the seeds of both life and death – its inner nature and the revival dating from the 1960s on the one hand, and on the other the pressures of intermarriage, migration and apathy.

Of all the subjects in this book, the story of the Welsh language most deserves a volume to itself, and indeed a whole six-volume series has been published simply on the social history of the language. Once Wales had lost the last of its princes in 1282, once it had been legally incorporated with English in 1536, the Welsh language and its culture were the sole distinguishing marks of Welsh identity. There were no national institutions such as law, universities and finance which sustained Scottish identity. There was no ongoing struggle for religious and social freedom like that at the heart of Irish identity. No wonder that the last line of the chorus of the national anthem, *Hen Wlad fy Nhadau,* is *O bydded i'r heniaith barhau* – long may the beloved language live.

4. Looking *for* A Welsh Capital

Machynlleth: Ancient Capital of Wales. This is surely the most misleading road-sign in Wales; this delightful little town could do without it. The claim can rest only on the fact that Owain Glyndŵr, who in 1404 had considerable power in Wales, held a parliament there. The claim could be a little better made for Harlech, where Glyndŵr held his second parliament, and which historians agree was the main centre of Glyndŵr's power from 1405 till 1409. (For another misleading municipal boast, see Carmarthen, whose welcome signs tell us that it is 'the Oldest Town in Wales' – a boast to which Caerwent has better title. It's true that today Caerwent is a village, but the Roman town on the site was earlier and much larger than Roman Maridunum.)

A capital city is not necessarily the largest or wealthiest city in a country. Glasgow is far bigger than Edinburgh but has never claimed to be Scotland's capital. Washington DC, Canberra, Brasilia and Ottawa are all smaller than the largest cities in their respective countries: the USA, Australia, Brazil and Canada. Nor does a capital have to be central. Essentially a capital is the seat of a country's government, not necessarily the centre of a country's culture.

In the high medieval period the Welsh lawbooks claimed special status for Aberffraw in Gwynedd, Dinefwr in Deheubarth and Mathrafal in Powys. Llywelyn the Great carried that claim in his preferred title, 'Prince of Aberffraw and Lord of Snowdon', though his poets optimistically proclaimed him to be 'king of Wales'. Historians today agree that these claims of status for Aberffraw, Dinefwr and Mathrafal are essentially medieval propaganda devised to support princely claims to power. It is clear from what we know of princely rule in Wales, and from the documents they issued, that their administrative rôle was carried out, not exactly on the hoof, but certainly in regular visits to the courts which existed in every cantref and commote.

When Wales was invaded from 1067 by barons and their knights who set up their own lordships in earlier Welsh administrative units, each with considerable independence from the Crown in London, the country was so morcellated that the very idea of a Welsh capital would have been laughable. When Edward I brought his idea of order to those parts of native Wales which had held out longest against him, he created two Principalities, North and South. The one was to be administered from Caernarfon, the other from Carmarthen. Communications were clearly far too difficult to make a single administrative centre easily practicable.

The first time that all Wales had an administrative centre of any kind was in 1472, and it was in England! In that year the Council for Wales and the Marches (Cheshire, Shropshire, Worcestershire and Herefordshire) was constituted, to be presided over by the king's eldest son, Prince of Wales – when there was one. The Council needed a location for its meetings. The choice of Ludlow reflects the geographical dilemma of administering Wales. Since the major valleys of Dee, Severn and Wye all flow England-wards, any centre of administration at that period was bound to be on the eastern edge of the country. It had to be somewhere equally accessible to Council members from all the lordships of Wales and the Marcher counties, as well as to the Prince of Wales and his entourage, based in London. Ludlow was a reasonably practical choice, and it flourished (with an intermission during the Commonwealth period) until the abolition of the Council in 1689.

The other possible choice of a convenient centre would have been Shrewsbury, whose loss to the Saxons had been lamented by the early poets of Powys under its ancient Welsh name *Pengwern*. Shrewsbury has long had Welsh connections: it had even been occupied in 1215 by Llywelyn the Great. When in the 1690s government restrictions on printing in the provinces had been removed, Thomas Jones saw the convenience of moving his printing press from London nearer Wales, and chose Shrewsbury. Later railway links to north, south and mid Wales meant the town was convenient for bodies such as the Church in Wales and the colleges of the University of Wales to hold meetings there. The late Professor T.J. Morgan even coined a Welsh verb, *mwythica*, from the town's modern Welsh name, Amwythig, meaning 'to go to Shrewsbury for a meeting'. Shrewsbury's Royal Infirmary, too, has long held a place in the medical history of mid-Wales.

As it was, the real capital of Wales was of course London. Not only because all governmental administration derived from London, but because it was a magnet drawing people from all over Wales, whether temporarily, like the drovers and the garden-women, or permanently. From the foundation of the Society of Ancient Britons in 1715, and especially the first Cymmrodorion Society of 1751 and the Gwyneddigion of 1770, London was the only real centre of Welsh intellectual life, with Carmarthen lagging a long way behind. Although printing had been firmly established in Wales before 1750, most of the important books in the Welsh language between 1750 and 1810 were printed in London – *Some Specimens of the Poetry of the Antient Welsh Bards* (1764), *Y Diddanwch Teuluaidd* (1763) and all the works of William Owen-Pughe, including his *Dictionary*, the poetry of Dafydd ap Gwilym and Llywarch Hen and the huge *Myvyrian Archaiology* (1801–7).

Even the first stone circle for the ceremony of the Gorsedd of Bards of the Island of Britain was laid out by Iolo Morganwg, not in Glamorgan but on Primrose Hill in 1792. He used a pocketful of pebbles for the task.

Despite dramatic changes in Welsh culture and the economy during the 19th century, there was no apparent concern among Welsh people that there should be a capital of Wales. After all, there was no legislative difference between Wales and England. The biggest change of the period as far as developing centres of Welsh life was the growth of Liverpool, with its large influx of people from north Wales and the consequent flourishing of numerous Welsh chapels. Liverpool's hospitals and its two biggest football clubs are still important in the life of north Wales. Meanwhile in the south Cardiff grew steadily from a village-sized borough to a major mercantile centre for shipping and coal exports, bringing much wealth to the area and challenging the status of Swansea and Merthyr Tydfil.

From the late 18th century there had been an increase in Welsh national self-consciousness, particularly due to the increasing religious differences between Wales and England. The growing railway network, which enabled book and periodical distribution and travel by nonconformist ministers, certainly helped the development of national self-knowledge. Religious differences also drove a developing allegiance to the Liberal party, as opposed to Toryism, which was perceived as an English phenomenon, associated with the landed gentry. From 1868 the peripatetic National Eisteddfod provided Welsh-speaking Wales with a cultural capital for a week every year, as it still does.

There began, too, an interest in establishing national institutions, particularly a university. When committees began to debate this possibility in the mid-19th century, the choice of site lay between Bangor and Cardiff – Bangor in Welsh-speaking heartland country, Cardiff in the burgeoning anglicised south-east. The near-penniless committee had its hand forced by the availability of a cheap building in Aberystwyth, equally accessible by recently arrived railway lines from every part of the country. Ironically the building had been created as a vast hotel for the expected influx of railway visitors, but the developer went bankrupt before the hotel could be used. Instead it became the home of the first University College of Wales in 1872.

It was not long before the second university college was established at Cardiff in 1883, much to the indignation of Swansea. Bangor succeeded in 1884. Cardiff was fortunate at this time in that much of its land belonged to the marquises of Bute. They were responsible firstly for the development of the docks and coal trade which enriched the town, and secondly for the development of parks and good urban buildings. When the town bought Cathays Park from the marquis in 1898, the land began to be exploited as the finest civic centre in Britain, with a splendid City Hall, later home to eleven marble statues of Welsh national heroes. Cardiff would gain further success with its recognition in 1905 as a city, with a Lord Mayor as its figurehead.

The next target after the university was the establishment of a national museum and gallery. Cardiff led the charge to house both institutions, but in the case of the library, despite the fine Free Library in the town, lost the argument. Wealthy Sir John Williams, Queen Victoria's physician, had secured ownership of unique collections of Welsh manuscripts and printed books, and was willing to endow the library – provided it was established at Aberystwyth. Cardiff, he felt, was a mongrel community, not nearly 'Welsh' enough. Both Library and Museum were given their royal charters in 1907.

However, Lloyd George's dominance in Welsh politics did not augur well for Cardiff, since his efforts to promote the 'Cymru Fydd' movement for Welsh home rule had been rebuffed in the 1890s by opposition from the south-east. When it was decided to set a precedent by holding an inauguration ceremony for the young Prince of Wales in 1911, it was inevitable that Lloyd George's powerful influence would ensure that the ceremony took place in Caernarvon. He was after all MP for the Carnarvon boroughs and a leading member of the Cabinet, and the first English Prince of Wales had been known as 'Edward of Caernarfon'.

Despite the existence in Cardiff of the Free Library and the National Museum, the success of the university and other colleges, despite the splendid Welsh National Opera company established after World War II, despite being the headquarters of the Welsh Arts Council and the BBC in Wales, Cardiff has only recently begun to look like the intellectual capital of Wales, as opposed to being its commercial and administrative capital.

That title might have been claimed in the mid-18th century for Carmarthen, with its radical theological college and its busy printing presses. It was outstripped by Swansea, with its Philosophical and Literary Society (1835) which three years later became the Royal Institution of South Wales. Swansea was the home of pioneer work in photography by Calvert Richard Jones and John Dillwyn-Llewelyn. The fine Glynn Vivian Art Gallery was opened in 1911; whether by chance or design it must have appeared as a rival of the recently opened National Museum and Gallery in Cardiff, which had not yet acquired the wonderful Gregynog collection of Impressionists' work. Swansea's Brangwyn Hall was the finest concert venue in the country. Most notably, perhaps, the Swansea of the

1930s produced the most famous of all Welsh poets, Dylan Thomas, his friend the composer Daniel Jones and a bevy of important painters. Aberystwyth, as home to the original University College, the National Library and the Centre for Advanced Welsh and Celtic Studies, is also claimed as the country's intellectual capital, though capital of scholarship would be an easier title to assert – no doubt to be dismissed by Cardiff.

In any case, Cardiff continued to attract other features with national status: the Central Welsh Board of Education in 1896, a Catholic cathedral in 1916, the Welsh Board of Health in 1919, the National War Memorial in 1928 (thanks to the *Western Mail*, itself claiming national status), and the city became a centre of radio broadcasting in 1937, although Swansea and Bangor too had studios. The creation of the Welsh Office in Cathays Park in 1965 was a major development on the road to devolution. Cardiff also developed as a sporting centre, especially since the holding of the Commonwealth Games in Cardiff in 1958. Rugby internationals were shared with Swansea until 1954, and soccer internationals have been played at both Swansea and Wrexham as well as Cardiff. Cardiff has also had to share the Glamorgan cricket team with Swansea and other Welsh centres. However, with the recent arrival of the English Test XI to play international matches at Sophia Gardens, Cardiff now has firm precedence in almost all sports, as had become clear when Wales hosted the Rugby World Cup in 1999 and when the Millennium Stadium was opened.

In retrospect it seems odd that it was a Conservative government which gave Cardiff the status of capital city of Wales in 1955. According to the *Encyclopaedia of Wales* (2008) the decision was due more to the number of marginal Conservative seats in and around the city than to any clear vision of what a

Welsh capital city might be. That the city's population also lacked vision was emphasised in 1997 when Cardiff voted against devolution for Wales, even though it should have been obvious even to the dullest voter that devolved government would be of massive benefit to the city. A capital city which votes against the improvement of its own status, both economic and political, was a weird entity indeed.

Perhaps Cardiff's failure to acknowledge its own position in Wales had already been reflected in the way that the University College of South Wales and Monmouthshire, to give it its original title, had almost from the first seemed to resent its status as a college in the federal University of Wales, and during the last decades of the 20th century it distanced itself further and further from the other colleges. In 2005 it finally gained status as an independent university granting its own degrees, a step rapidly imitated by Swansea, Aberystwyth and Bangor, leaving the University of Wales a shadow of its former self.

For a brief moment after the successful vote for devolution in 1997 it looked as though Swansea rather than Cardiff might benefit. The inability of Cardiff to agree reasonable terms for the use of the fine City Hall as a home – at least temporary – for the nascent Welsh Assembly led the then Secretary for Wales, Ron Davies, to canvass Swansea as a possible residence for the Assembly. Swansea had after all voted in favour of devolution. But the idea of a parliament forty miles from the capital city was never really a starter, so the Assembly was established in Cardiff Bay. Swansea was bought off, so to speak, with the National Swimming Centre (2003) and the National Maritime Museum (2005). In any case all had changed by 3 March 2011, when the capital voted by a thumping majority in favour of giving the Assembly extended powers to legislate. At last Cardiff deserved its title as capital of Wales.

It was always inevitable that Cardiff would have a complex relationship with the rest of Wales. Closely linked to London by train, it was never easy to establish it as a centre for publication of a national newspaper. The *Western Mail* does its best these days to justify the title, but north Wales remains loyal to the *(Liverpool) Daily Post*, insofar as people buy anything other than London papers. BBC Wales and the Welsh-language channel S4C are both well-established in Cardiff, but the recent freakish multiplication of TV channels and VHF radio stations, not to mention the mushrooming internet, inevitably turns people's eyes and ears eastwards.

As Cardiff had developed, it looked inland as far as Merthyr Tudful and the Rhondda, but hardly further. Its position in trade and commerce, especially shipping, inevitably meant turning its back on Wales to a large degree. Its mixed, indeed cosmopolitan, population laid it open to assertions that the city was not really Welsh at all. Indeed, in 1911 a larger percentage of Cardiff's population were foreign-born than anywhere in Britain except London. It was inevitable that the mixed origins of Cardiff's population would provoke resentment and suspicion, hence Sir John Williams's insistence on the National Library being at Aberystwyth. Hence too the opinion relayed by my Caernarfon-born landlady in 1962 that the people of her town were furious when Cardiff was made capital; was Caernarfon not the Welshest town in Wales? Had it not hosted the Investiture of 1911? But the decision was always inevitable. As Wales gradually became a nation once again, it needed a capital, and it was always going to be Cardiff.

5. Looking *for* Welsh Castles

The arrival of the Normans in Wales from 1067 onwards must have been a traumatic experience for the Welsh. They were used to living lightly on the land, building their houses and churches from wood; even the halls in which their princes dispensed justice were of timber. Individuals who had crossed Offa's Dyke to England and beyond, or who had sailed to Ireland, certainly saw buildings of stone. But stone buildings from the Welsh past, whether hill-forts with their mighty ramparts or the Roman walls of Caerwent and the great bathhouse at Caerleon, were all crumbling ruins.

But from 1067 the Normans were pressing all along the Welsh border, led by powerful men, friends of the new king of England, empowered by him to carve out lands for themselves in Welsh territory. William had immediately begun the building of the White Tower in London, a symbol of his power and authority. His followers replaced the Old English landowning aristocracy, so many of whom had fallen at Hastings. They began building castles which must have startled and impressed the English peasant population. Only a very few earth castles had been built in England prior to 1066, on French models. But now the castle was the weapon of colonisation.

This was especially the case in Wales where the castle was not simply a military base, but a potential centre of borough development in a country which had no towns. There would have to be housing for the lord's followers and camp-followers: craftsmen, suppliers of provisions, and a church. Mills were necessary for grinding corn and fulling wool. Local land was put under more intensive cultivation and orchards planted.

Womenfolk, most likely locally recruited, would provide wives and servants. Both men and women would be recruited or forced to work on building the great earth mounds, the mottes, which were the early castles. Some mottes may have been temporary staging posts in the back-and-forth process of colonisation and conquest. Many can be seen well away from any sign of present-day settlements, having entirely lost their own history, while others still stand in or close to their settlements.

Soon the Normans, especially in the south, were building in more durable materials. Stone castles, churches and town walls sprouted, first along the border and the south coast, then in more modest form across the north and west, especially as the Welsh themselves learnt to build castles and churches, sometimes employing foreign builders. With the Edwardian conquests of 1277 and 1283 came the zenith of castle-building in Conwy, Caernarfon, Harlech and Beaumaris. It is a paradox of history that these alien buildings intended to cow the Welsh into submission have become a pride of Welsh tourism. Thomas Pennant, major Welsh antiquarian and scholar of the late 18th century, called Caernarfon 'the magnificent badge of our subjection'.

Those four great Edwardian castles hardly need further promotion. Often thought of as a group, in many ways they are quite different. Each is well adapted to its position: Beaumaris and Caernarfon on virtually level sites, one symmetrical but unfinished, the other a bravura embodiment of imperial rule. Conwy, originally intended as Edward's capital for his Principality of North Wales, has a more dominant position than the other two, while Harlech on its mighty crag is the most imperious of all.

It should be remembered that the sites of each of the four great Gwynedd castles had a previous life and identity of its own. Llan-faes in Anglesey had been a small Welsh borough, which Edward relocated to Newborough so that Beaumaris could be built. Caernarfon had Roman connections as well as a motte. Edward's builders celebrated the Roman and imperial connection with banded stonework and Roman eagles. At Conwy, Llywelyn the Great (d. 1240) had founded and endowed the Cistercian abbey in whose church he and his sons, Dafydd and Gruffudd, had been buried. Edward moved the abbey up the Conwy valley to Maenan, allowing the monks to take their founder's remains with them. Llywelyn's coffin is to be seen in Llanrwst church. Harlech rock, for its part, is celebrated as one of the courts of the giant Bendigeidfran, sovereign of the Island of the Mighty, in the tragic tale of his sister Branwen.

Each of the four castles also had an afterlife, so to speak. Two of them played dramatic parts in the great 1400 rebellion of Owain Glyndŵr. In 1401 the Tudor brothers Rhys and Gwilym from Anglesey, marked men because of their association with Glyndŵr, brazenly walked into Conwy Castle at Easter when the garrison was in church and held it for several months. They finally surrendered it in exchange for royal pardons, which did not extend to some of their associates, who were handed over for execution. Harlech was besieged and captured by Glyndŵr's forces in 1404 and it became a centre of his rule in north Wales until the garrison was starved out in 1409.

Nor was that the end of Harlech's battles. During the Wars of the Roses, that long and bitter struggle for the crown of England, Harlech was held for the Lancastrians from 1461 till 1468, when its surrender left Edward IV in apparent control of the realm. Then after nearly two centuries of obscurity, it was garrisoned for Charles I against the parliamentary forces who in 1646–7 drove up the west Wales coast taking castle after castle; Harlech was the last to surrender in that campaign. When the second Civil War broke out in 1648 Beaumaris was the last castle in Wales to surrender in war.

Less well-known than Edward's masterpieces, but equal in strength and magnificence, are the mighty baronial castles of south Wales. Against the four Gwynedd castles may be set the five splendid castles of Chepstow, Pembroke, Cardiff, Caerphilly and Raglan. Scarcely less splendid are Cydweli and Cilgerran. Whereas both Edward's last four castles and his earlier ring of stone at Aberystwyth, Builth, Flint and Rhuddlan were specifically designed with imperial conquest in mind, the great castles of the south were the work of individual barons. They were the centres of separate lordships, built not only to dominate the local Welsh but in egotistical competition with each other. In the case of Caerphilly, Gilbert de Clare was particularly concerned to warn off the ambitions of Llywelyn ap Gruffudd, Prince of Wales, and may secretly have fancied himself as powerful as king Edward, a serious mistake.

Although I have sought to emphasise differences between the four great Edwardian castles of Gwynedd, they nevertheless resemble each other in being contemporary, built within a few years from 1283 and little altered later. The great baronial castles, on the other hand, apart from Caerphilly, were each built over many years to plans which altered as they grew. Perhaps they have not wholly received the honour they deserve because they differ so considerably in date and style. The drawback for non-Cadw castles like Pembroke and Cardiff is that they do not share in the extensive publicity which Cadw generates. Folk who buy an annual Cadw pass (good for England and Scotland as well) still have to pay to enter Cardiff, Pembroke, and several other major castles in separate ownership, such as Powis Castle and Penrhyn (National Trust), Caldicot (Monmouth County Council) and Picton (private trust).

These baronial castles, then, are extraordinary in their variety. For sheer magnificence of defensive design few castles can equal Gilbert de Clare's Caerphilly. As well as the extensive moats and lake which surround the whole, the main entrance is defended by double bridges and gates. Almost every Welsh castle succumbed to attack at some stage, but not Caerphilly, though assaulted by the Welsh in 1295 and 1316. Glyndŵr's rebels seem to have steered clear of it, and it played little part in the Civil War. Pembroke likewise never succumbed to Welsh attack, though on one occasion that was only because the townsfolk gave Llywelyn the Great £100 to stay away. Pembroke's position at the seaward end of a fine ridge, further than any other castle from the princes of Deheubarth, as well as the daunting strength of its colossal keep, helped secure its position. Only in 1648 did Pembroke endure a serious siege, when Cromwell in person attacked the renegade garrison and forced their surrender. Other fine Pembrokeshire castles include Manorbier and Carew.

Cardiff and Raglan have some faint resemblance in that both became palaces rather than castles. Cardiff certainly began as a fine motte with a splendid shell keep, in the middle of the ruins of a large Roman fort. This first castle endured the famous onslaught of Ifor Bach of the mountain lordship of Senghennydd, who in 1158 kidnapped his overlord, Earl William of Glamorgan and carried him off to the hills. Cardiff escaped attack during the Civil War, and instead was developed in fits and starts into one of the most extraordinary combination of buildings in Britain. Apart from the original keep, it has later medieval towers and a hall with some Elizabethan alterations, original landscaping (now largely vanished) by Capability Brown and uniquely extraordinary Victorian alterations and lavish decorated work by William Burges. The whole is surrounded by a colossal re-creation of the original Roman fort on the ruins of the ancient walls.

Raglan was to be the last medieval Welsh castle. In 1432 work began formidably enough with the building of the huge, well-defended Yellow Tower of Gwent by William ap Thomas. Further developments by his son William Herbert and later descendants added two fine paved courts and a magnificent series of domestic rooms which must have been far more comfortable and better furnished than earlier medieval castles; indeed, Raglan became more palace than castle. Since it is later than the period of the Conquest, Raglan never needed to shelter a borough beneath its walls, and although some damage was done during the Civil War siege of 1646, the ruins are among the finest in the land. Visitors to Raglan should not simply just enjoy the fine rural views in all directions; they should also allow their imaginations to see orchards and gardens, arable enclosures and grazing sheep and cattle, with fishponds and working mills, all worked by local peasants for the benefit of the lordship.

What then of mid Wales, which has not hitherto been mentioned? The shattered ruins of Aberystwyth and the heaving earthworks that remain at Builth (both Edwardian) do not bear comparison, in their present state, with any of the castles mentioned above. There were of course plenty of motte-and-bailey and ring-work castles scattered through the land as the Norman assaults surged and retreated. Quite the most splendid of the castles of mid Wales is Powis Castle, known from its fine stonework as Castell Coch. But since Powys, like Chirk further north and Picton in the southwest, became a stately home and was always inhabited, it is referred to in another chapter.

Instead we turn to a final group of castles which have received much attention from scholars in recent years after long years of neglect – the castles of the Welsh Princes. So different were the traditions and practices of Welsh and Norman warfare that it took some time for the Welsh to start building motte-and-bailey castles. To put it simply, the Welsh saw themselves using tip-and-run or guerilla tactics in war; they lacked the Normans' resources for hold-and-fight. A Welsh prince's first defence was his war-band of experienced warriors, not a stone wall. But from 1116, the date of the first recorded Welsh motte, Welsh castle-building increased until Rhys ap Gruffudd – the Lord Rhys – felt able in 1171 to build in stone at Cardigan. He may already have started work in stone at Dinefwr, but neither record nor wall of that date survives.

Because castles changed hands, were damaged and rebuilt, the status of a Welsh-built castle is not always easy to determine. For example, the splendid castle of Carreg Cennen, near Llandeilo, must originally have been the work of Rhys ap Gruffudd or his family, but all the surviving stonework is post-1278, the work of the English. The northern castles of the two Llywelyns: Llywelyn the Great at Dolwyddelan, Dolbadarn, Cricieth, Castell y Bere and possibly Carndochan, his grandson Llywelyn the Last at Ewloe and Dolforwyn, were not much interfered with by the conquerors. In the south Rhys ap Gruffudd built additional castles at Rhaeadr and the Dyfi estuary, and captured and almost certainly strengthened the castles at Nevern and Llandovery. His descendants built at Trefilan, Dryslwyn and Newcastle Emlyn. To the east, the princes of Powys built at Welshpool (Powis Castle) and Dinas Brân, while in the south-east a number of small castles are attributed to the lords of Machen (Castell Meredydd) and Senghennydd (Morgraig).

Welsh-built castles share a number of features. As one might expect from princes who never had the resources of an English king or of barons such as William Marshal and Gilbert de Clare, they are smaller, and show signs of economy in building, most obviously a shortage of good mortar. Also, as one might expect in a time when the Anglo-Normans held much of lowland

Wales, Welsh castles tended to be perched on high crags. Even seaside Cricieth sits atop a splendid rocky hump. These were easier to defend than lowland castles but not so easy to keep supplied with water.

Though the Welsh princes certainly took to castle-building, and developed considerable expertise in the use of siege weapons, it seems clear from the documents of the time that, at least in the case of the princes of Gwynedd and probably beyond to east and south, the Welsh princes preferred their courts to their castles for ordinary use. These courts were much less formidable than any castle, as is clear from the modest remains which have been revealed at Rhosyr in Anglesey and Abergwyngregyn in Caernarfonshire, and from the size of the timber halls which Edward I carried to his new castles at Harlech and Conwy and re-erected there.

There is a handful of folly-castles in Wales, built usually in Victorian imitation of the medieval to satisfy the vanity of men with huge sums of money to spend. Several are outstanding of their kind. In south Wales there is Cyfarthfa Castle, really a castellated mansion, the creation of the wealth of William Crawshay and his giant ironworks. It now contains a delightfully old-fashioned museum and is well worth a visit. Near Cardiff is the remarkable Castell Coch, a Bute-Burges rebuild of a medieval castle of possible Welsh origin. It is a favourite location for Ruritanian film-settings. In north Wales there is Gwrych castle, an extraordinary excrescence distractingly visible from the A55, now derelict. Even larger is the colossal Penrhyn Castle at Llandygái near Bangor, splendidly sited above the Menai Strait. Penrhyn was built on the wealth of the Pennant family's slave plantations of the West Indies and the near slavery of the local slate industry.

Readers interested in visiting Welsh castles are strongly advised to join Cadw, or if from England, English Heritage; membership will soon pay for itself. If you have already visited the great (and fee-paying) castles, then it is more important to invest in maps. Castles are not always easy to track down. The great ruins of Flint, for example, can be seen across the town from the western slope, but are difficult to find thanks to the confusing one-way system in the town and the lack of signs for motorists. Sycharth, a magnificent motte-and-bailey complete with fishponds, famous for its association with Owain Glyndŵr and its description by the poet Iolo Goch, is not easy to locate west of Oswestry in greenest Wales.

Some castles, for example the great castle at Denbigh, have open gates in winter but a fee has to be paid in summer. The Three Castles of Gwent – Grosmont, Skenfrith and White Castle, can be visited in a day by walking or an afternoon by car, without having to pay a penny. Dinas Brân and Carndochan are free too, but involve some serious uphill walking. Ewloe requires a fair walk from the badly-signed Wepre Country Park, but is well worth the effort.

There are indeed more castles to visit than can be listed in a brief chapter such as this. There are several useful books listing sixty to eighty worthwhile castles, while for home study the website http://www.castlewales.com/ offers wonderful pictures and good descriptions. Cadw guidebooks are always of the highest quality. Enjoy the castles of Wales; castles and chapels are important elements in the Welsh landscape. Enjoy, too, their place in the history of art in Wales. First portrayed in 18th-century engravings by the Buck brothers, Welsh castles became a major element in landscape art, never more so than in the work of Richard Wilson and J.M.W. Turner.

6. Looking *for* Welsh Churches

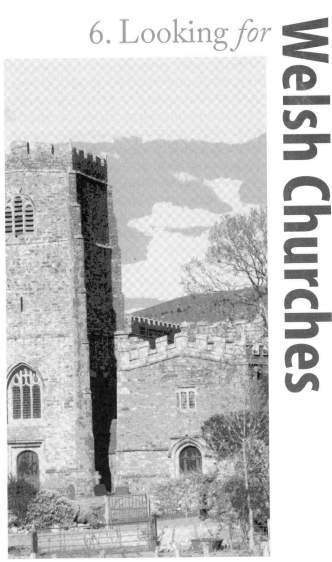

You might well suppose Wales has little to offer by way of historic churches in comparison with the ecclesiastical riches of England. If so, you would be quite wrong. Historic, beautiful, charming churches in Wales are too numerous to list in a chapter. It's true that Wales cannot possibly compete with that great chain of English cathedrals from Durham to Lincoln to Norwich to Canterbury to Exeter, to name only a few. Then what of Norfolk, a single county with more medieval churches than all Wales? What of the pre-1066 Anglo-Saxon churches, not nearly so well-known as they should be even in England: Bradford-on-Avon, Escomb, Earls Barton and Bradwell-on-Sea.

It is indeed true that Wales has only one great cathedral and not a single church from before 1066, save only a fragment of Presteigne parish church, right on the English border. Nevertheless, Wales can offer many real surprises. There are standing stones with Christian crosses and inscriptions, others elaborately or simply carved, not to mention holy wells of immemorial date; Holywell and Llangybi (near Pwllheli) are particularly worth visiting. There is some fine medieval stained glass in north Wales; Llanrhaeadr-yng-Nghinmeirch, between Denbigh and Ruthin, has as fine an east window as any parish church in Britain; Gresford's windows are a delight, and there are other scattered gems. Other Welsh treasures are the comparatively large number of surviving medieval oak screens and rood-lofts scattered across the country.

The dedicated church-crawler will of course come across the occasional frustration, especially the locked door with no directions on where to find the key. Thus the great Norman chancel at Ewenny Priory, the only fortified monastic centre in

Britain, is not easy to visit, nor is Carmarthen's historic parish church, St Peter's. One can naturally sympathise with the problems of theft and vandalism faced both by isolated and by urban churches. Fortunately there are still many dedicated members of congregations who give time to keep their churches accessible. But for fear of thieves like those who stole armour from lonely Pilleth Church, moveable treasures are not mentioned here.

Naturally the six cathedral churches – St David's, Llandaff, Brecon, Newport, Bangor and St Asaph are all open daily, listed here in my own debatable order of preference: St David's is the only Welsh cathedral which compares with what one might call England's first division, with Llandaff a worthy runner-up. What makes a cathedral great? It has to be capacious; its nave should derive from a single period, it must have a variety of subordinate styles and complexity of plan, it must have an inner spiritual warmth. It should have good monuments, but not so many that it becomes a mausoleum, and it should have green space around it. Ideally it should have a vaulted nave; St David's has all those features save the vaulted nave, but compensates with a magnificent timber roof of superb complexity, and there is good vaulting in subordinate chapels. The choir has fine misericords and other medieval carved work. The restoration of the medieval St Mary's college and the recent remodelling of the ancient cloister and the shrine of David are superb.

The other cathedrals in Wales all have features to recommend them. Llandaff is exceptional for its double recovery, first from the neglect of the 18th century, which left the nave roofless, and then from the major havoc of a WWII bomb. The restoration work, the Memorial and Lady Chapels, the great Epstein Christ in Majesty, the pre-Raphaelite stained glass, the modern military chapel – all give Llandaff much of the star quality a cathedral should possess. Brecon, originally a major priory church and retaining the whole range of its subordinate monastic buildings, has enough complexity to warrant approval. Newport has good Norman arcades; Bangor was the burial place of Owain Gwynedd and holds the splendid medieval wood-carving known as the Mostyn Christ. St Asaph, now very much a memorial to Bishop William Morgan, translator of the Welsh Bible, has fine medieval choir stalls.

We turn to monastic foundations. Pre-Norman Welsh monasticism left no buildings, but lovely situations. Few sites were abandoned; the Normans turned some to collegiate churches, some directly to parish churches. At first they preferred to establish urban priories, offshoots of French abbeys, close to their castles – hence Chepstow, Abergavenny, Ewenni, Kidwelly and many more. Llantony, north of Abergavenny, is more special, founded by a knight in remote, beautiful countryside. The ruins deserve a visit, as does the tiny bar in the medieval cellar of the abbot's house.

Change came with the arrival of the Cistercians direct from France. They established a chain of abbeys, some of them endowed by Welsh princes, others by Marcher lords. In the west and north particularly, the Cistercians quickly went native, copying Welsh and Welsh/Latin manuscripts, acting as emissaries for their princes, whom they honoured with burial in their churches. These were financially poor by comparison with the great abbeys of England, let alone France, and most fell into ruins while others disappeared entirely. Tintern has the most complete and spectacular church ruins, while Margam has not only its chapter-house and much altered church, but a magnificent collection of early carved stones and crosses. Valle Crucis near Llangollen is a delight. Some Welsh visitors may feel more at home among the humbler but numinous fragments of Cymer, Cwm-hir and above all Strata Florida; sparse though the wreckage is, the associations of the place with its unrivalled literary associations and the extraordinary peace of the valley are enchanting. Two other monastic sites worth visiting are Talley Abbey deep in rural Carmarthenshire and St Dogmaels near Cardigan.

There are many major parish churches to be found in Wales, especially within reach of the border, in wealthier country. They run from Cardiff's St John's via Chepstow, Usk (originally a convent church), Monmouth, Abergavenny and Skenfrith; then northward via Old Radnor and Meifod to the splendid parish churches (especially the towers) of the north-east – Ruthin, Mold, Gresford and above all, Wrexham. Indeed the north-east holds many other treasures: Llangollen, with its carved roof rivalling St David's itself; the classicism of Worthenbury, rare in Wales; the painted interior of Rug Chapel, the timberwork at Cilcain and the restored peace of Llangar.

One cannot describe these fascinating churches in a short chapter, so let me choose Abergavenny. For a start, the medieval tithe-barn next door has been restored as an excellent visitors' centre with exhibition. The church's elegant nave is rather chilly to the eye, but the medieval choir stalls are special. Above all there is an extraordinary collection of monumental tombs from the 13th century to the 17th. There is nothing like it in any other British parish church. Unique too is the colossal medieval oak figure of Jesse, not a monument but once the foundation figure of a sculptured Jesse Tree which bore images of his descendants. It was a family tree in reverse, once reaching a climax with the figure of Christ. All the other figures have vanished, but the Abergavenny Jesse is still a giant medieval masterpiece.

These great border churches have an honoured place in the Welsh landscape, but there are other, more secret foundations which have special stories to tell. Here and there across the countryside, sometimes tucked away in a dell, sometimes on a mountain's shoulder, are real Welsh treasures, of which a brief chapter like this can only mention a few. For example, after a morning visit to Abergavenny, the road north to Hereford runs through Llanfihangel Crucorney. Turn left there, and follow signs along the tiny road upwards onto the Black Mountain; it will lead you past a holy well to Patrisio, with its richly carved medieval screen, its two medieval stone altars and breathtaking views. Back into the valley, bear left and follow signs to Cwmyoy. This medieval church was not built on a rock as Christ advocated but on a seriously unstable slope, so that there isn't a right-angle in the building. Further up the valley is Llanthony, already mentioned.

Just west of Cardiff is the St Fagans Museum of Welsh Life, among whose many buildings is the re-created church of Llandeilo Tal-y-bont. This stood for centuries on the floodplain of the River Llwchwr, and was abandoned. Removal and restoration brought the discovery of medieval wall-paintings, preserved elsewhere. In the Vale of Glamorgan lies Llantwit Major, one of those many churches whose site is much more ancient than its splendidly quirky medieval building, with some good early carved crosses. The same antiquity is shared by many Welsh country churches; which often retained their dedications to a host of Welsh and a few Irish saints – Teilo, Illtud, Gwenffrewi (Winifred), Padarn, Beuno, Ffraid, to name only the best-known. Pembrokeshire has a number of these ecclesiastical gems, among them Nevern, Llanwnda, Manordeifi Old Church and the remarkable early 20th-century re-creation at Llandeloy. The county also has two fine urban churches at Tenby and Haverfordwest.

Further north, Ceredigion has five attractive churches,

Mwnt, Llanwenog, Llanddewibrefi, Llanfihangel-y-Creuddyn and Llanbadarn Fawr. Mid Wales offers Llangurig, Llanidloes, Welshpool (if you can get in), and the lovely Radnor churches of Llananno, Llanbister and Old Radnor, the finest of them. On the west coast of Gwynedd are gems at Tywyn (one of the oldest in the country), Llanegryn, Llangelynin, Llanaber (Barmouth), Llanddwywe and Llandanwg. Further east, hidden in the folds of the Berwyn range is Pennant Melangell, splendidly restored. Its unique medieval shrine is visited all year round by pilgrims to this lonely, lovely valley.

Northwards to the Conwy Valley, one can spend time first at Llanrwst, with its splendid screen and extraordinary Gwydir chapel, then to Trefriw to climb the giddy road to Llanrhychwyn, a tiny church on the Snowdonia massif. Joan, Lady of Wales and wife of Llywelyn the Great, loathed the steep climb and persuaded her husband to found a more convenient church by his hunting lodge at Trefriw. Further north are lonely Llangelynin and lowland Gyffin, near Conwy. Eastwards then to the Vale of Clwyd, with Llanfair-yng-Nghinmeirch (already mentioned), Ruthin and Tremeirchion.

Turning westwards, south of Caernarfon lies the lonely, disused but well-cared-for church of Llanfaglan, the great church at Clynnog and down the Llŷn peninsula, via Pistyll to Llanengan and three-naved Llangwnnadl, and ultimately to Aberdaron and Bardsey Island. The peninsula doesn't look big on a map, but it demands a full day at the very least.

That leaves Anglesey. The island once had some eighty medieval parishes, and at least forty churches retain some or nearly all of their medieval fabric. The two largest medieval foundations are Holyhead (set in a Roman fort, splendidly carved outside, difficult for admission) and Beaumaris, which seems a completely English outpost (with misericords) until you discover the grave slab of Llywelyn's princess Joan, daughter of King John, known in her lifetime as the Lady of Wales. More 'Welsh' in nature are the little churches scattered hither and yon through the island, from Llangadwaladr in the west to Llaneilian in the north-east. Finest of all is Penmon, twelfth-century church of the Welsh princes, with its holy well, St Seiriol's cell and the Augustinian priory ruins, fish-pond and the slightly later dovecot, and above all the stone carvings in the old nave. Penmon is, to me at least, the supreme gem of Welsh gems.

Visitors to Wales may find the presence of chapels more striking than churches, since there are so many of them – far more than in England. A small Welsh village may have three chapels, while in a town there may be three chapels in a single street. There were always going to be too many, since five denominations competed for attention: the Baptists, the Congregationalists (these two strong in the south), the Calvinistic Methodists (the largest denomination, stronger in the north), the Wesleyan Methodists and (in south Ceredigion and a few towns) the Unitarians. Moreover, in the towns the denominations had two languages to cater for, and rather than two congregations sharing the same building, there tended to be duplication

Why five denominations? The Baptists broke with Anglicanism by prioritising baptism as the total immersion of believers, not infants. Baptists and Congregationalists both emphasised the supremacy of the individual and independent congregation. Methodists broke with Anglicanism because it did not offer a sufficient emphasis on spiritual and emotional experience. Most followed the Calvinist teachings of George Whitefield and the Welsh Revivalists; others preferred the gentler theology of John Wesley. Unitarians reject the doctrine of the Trinity and the divinity of Christ.

of buildings. More complicated still, in some areas the Baptists divided into sects, each needing its own building.

Visible though they are, chapels do not attract visitors in the way that churches do. People unfamiliar with nonconformist culture cannot be expected to fully grasp their significance. This is a pity, because some of the finest 19th-century architecture in Wales is that of the best chapels. True, they are rarely open to visitors, for the good reason that their interiors do not contain the kind of medieval work that attracts visitors, nor do they usually provide weekday services or serve as places for private devotion. The weekday religious and social life of chapels uses their own vestries. Typically in the countryside a chapel complex will have three linked buildings, the chapel itself, the *tŷ capel* or caretaker's house and the hall or vestry.

Country chapels owe much of their attractiveness to their modesty. They were built by their members, most of whom found it easier to provide materials and labour than cash. Indeed, the earliest surviving meeting houses from the 17th century don't look like chapels at all. Fine early examples can be found at Meillionen near Glasbury south-west of Hay-on-Wye, tiny Carmel, Nantmel in Radnorshire, Soar-y-Mynydd south-east of Tregaron and the restored Unitarian chapel in the grounds of the museum at St Fagans.

It was in towns that congregations began in the 19th century to vie with each other for the growing splendour of their buildings, with flurries of Corinthian capitals, pilasters, rose windows, stained glass and gothic tracery – even spires, like Morriston's Tabernacl (no -e; this is a Welsh-speaking congregation) or St Andrew's Roath, Cardiff, with its church-like title and twin towers. Whether in town or country, many chapels wear their brief histories on their foreheads, so to speak. A slate inscription will give the dates of first foundation, remodelling, rebuilding or restoration.

Wales was so well-provided with churches and chapels that modern architects have had little scope for work in this field, except of course for restoration. There are some splendid exceptions, for example the Arts and Crafts buildings of the Caldey Island monastery. Examples of modern chapels can be found at Llanystumdwy, where Moriah is a fine Presbyterian chapel designed by the agnostic Clough Williams-Ellis in 1936, and in Wrexham's Capel-y-Groes. Then there is the extraordinary Roman Catholic church of Our Lady Star of the Sea at Amlwch, built in the 1930s by an Italian engineer.

Rural and (in places like the Rhondda and Blaenau Ffestiniog) urban depopulation, as well as the general secularisation of society, has left many churches and chapels without a congregation. No fewer than 22 rural treasures have been given to the Friends of Friendless Churches, whose excellent website gives details of each. There has been a steady increase in the sale of chapels and churches for other purposes, not to mention the transfer of some buildings to other denominations. Thus Aberaeron's Roman Catholics use a former Wesleyan chapel, while Manod church in Blaenau Ffestiniog is now an Orthodox church. Mostly however, abandoned churches and chapels have been pulled down or secularised, often as houses. In Aberystwyth, for example, I know of at least three chapels which have disappeared entirely, one of them burnt down. Another has become a pub, with much of its decoration and many fittings still in place; the third became a now-defunct garage. The town's oldest chapel building is now the national headquarters of the Welsh women's movement, Merched y Wawr. In the south Wales valleys scores of chapels have been pulled down or recycled, and serious efforts are being made by Cadw to record them before all traces vanish. They are a shrinking cloud of witnesses to the faith which gave life, form and vigour to Welsh culture.

7. Looking *for* The Great Houses of Wales

The Welsh philosopher and reformer Dr Richard Price was once travelling from London for his annual visit to his family near Bridgend, and to preside at the Masonic Lodge there. It was the late 18th century, and Price was accompanied on his leisurely journey by an English friend. At one point, before they had reached Wales, the friend said:

> 'I suppose, Sir, that in Wales we shall not see many gentlemen's houses.'
> 'On the contrary, Sir,' was the reply. 'In Wales every house is a gentleman's house.'

There's a world of significance in that little exchange. Price was of course putting his snobbish friend in the wrong and asserting his own Welsh pride. He is also alluding wryly to the well-known Welsh passion for genealogy and the fact that far more Welshmen claimed gentle descent than could possibly demonstrate it financially. Price's reply was the best way he had of glossing over the fact that Wales was a poorer country than England. English cartoonists and wags had been making jokes about Welsh poverty for centuries prior to Price's mild witticism.

There were in fact hundreds of gentlemen's houses in Wales, though not often on the same scale of wealth and elegance as the great homes of England. Through English eyes many were little more than yeomen's houses. Wales, though it once had the virtual palace of Raglan, now has no Blenheim, no Chatsworth. Only Penrhyn Castle, owned by the National Trust since 1951 and described by experts as 'one of the most enormous houses in Britain', can compare in scale with the great English behemoths in size, if not beauty.

From 1880 onwards the number of great houses in Wales diminished rapidly, especially after the Great War. One of the saddest books on any Welsh topic is Thomas Lloyd's *The Lost Houses of Wales*, now out of print, which lists over 350 country houses across Wales which fell into ruin, were destroyed by fire or deliberately smashed by their disillusioned owners or purchasers. The list seems never-ending: Ruperra Castle, the Adam house at Wenvoe, Baron Hill (ruins), Edwinsford (ruins), Bronwydd (ruined, now demolished), Ynysymaengwyn (deliberately burnt), Stackpole Court (demolished by its owner in a fit of despair), Hafod (ruins), Middleton Hall (its levelled site now home to the National Botanic Garden of Wales), Downing Hall (vanished), Piercefield (a wartime artillery practice target) – these are only a few of the many lost mansions of Wales. A small but ironic fact is that the folly towers of Middleton and Derry Ormond are now listed buildings while their mansions have long gone. In other places valuable estate lands have survived the demolition of the great house, as at Stackpole near Pembroke, where the National Trust maintains and keeps open a fine stretch of coastline, and at Dolaucothi, where the house was already beyond rescue and had to be demolished when the Trust acquired the estate, but where the gold mine is open to the public from early March till the end of October.

Many of these losses were inevitable. Not every great house was an architectural gem, nor was every one furnished to a high standard. One reason why there were so many losses in Wales was that the value of Welsh estates tended to be less than English estates. Whereas it was the post-1945 taxes on top of wartime losses which crushed so many English landowners, in Wales much damage had already been done by 1920 through death duties, agricultural decline and the loss of heirs in the Great War. Many Welsh landowners had insufficient resources on which they could survive. Additionally, the Welsh landowning class felt itself rejected by the bulk of the Welsh people, who had become Nonconformist in religion and voted Liberal to oust their superiors, not only from Parliament but even from the County Councils created in 1889.

Nevertheless some fine houses survived the waves of losses. The most fortunate cases were those still in good condition when given to the National Trust by owners. The gem of them all is Powis Castle, Welshpool, acquired in 1952. Here is a medieval castle splendidly adapted as a home, with its fine library, long gallery and main living rooms in magnificent condition, and outside, the finest historic garden in Britain. Another such is Chirk Castle (acquired in 1978), right on the English border, which like Powys metamorphosed slowly from the medieval period onwards. A third great house in every sense is Plas Newydd, Anglesey, superbly situated on the Menai Straits, acquired in 1976.

Other great houses only survived ruination by a whisker. By the mid-20th century Erddig near Wrexham. had cracked down the middle thanks to mining subsidence, so the rain poured in. The garden was a jungle and few people realised that the owner was still in residence, occupying the butler's pantry. Fortunately the 2,000-acre estate was still intact. The Trust was able to accept the gift by selling land close to Wrexham for building, thus providing a dowry. Enormous expenditure brought the house and garden back to splendid condition, and Erddig is cherished particularly by those who love the exemplary way in which the servants were treated. Another splendid house which survived severe vicissitudes is Tredegar House, Newport. Once the home of Wales's richest family, the Morgans, the last of them lived a playboy lifestyle before leaving the house to its fate, empty of all its possessions. It was taken over by a Roman Catholic school and then by Newport Council, who did their best to restore it before leasing it to the National Trust.

A story as remarkable as that of Erddig is the complex of castle, mansion and picturesque landscaped park of Dinefwr, Llandeilo. The castle is closely associated with one of the greatest medieval Welsh princes, Rhys ap Gruffudd ('the Lord Rhys') and the estate with Sir Rhys ap Thomas, who in 1485 helped ensure Henry Tudor's victory at Bosworth. The castle ruins are splendid, the house less distinguished but still a worthy representative of its type with a most attractive interior. The magnificent park and ancient oak woods are home to herds of fallow deer and White Park cattle.

Death duties, sales of land and dwindling resources forced Richard, Lord Dynevor, to give up after a long struggle, and he began to sell almost all the assets. Fortunately the medieval castle and bluebell woods went to the region's Wildlife Trust and Cadw eventually took charge of the castle ruins, but the mansion, its fine courtyards and outbuildings and the Home Farm with part of the park were all sold off. The herd of White Park cattle, the last in Wales, was also sold. In the mid-1980s Lord Dynevor managed to interest the National Trust in what remained in his hands, namely the rest of the park and woodlands. The Trust committee from its Swindon headquarters were not initially keen, but one member swung them round to realise the historic significance of the site, ending his peroration with a rendition of Thomas Love Peacock's well-known verses, 'The War Song of Dinas Fawr'. But the house had changed hands, it had been occupied for a period by squatters, it even lost the lead from the roof.

One by one the National Trust was able to buy the assets: the house itself and its fine inner courtyard, the Home Farm and the rest of the park, while the descendants of the White Park cattle were brought back to Dinefwr by the original purchaser, where they flourish again alongside the deer. The mansion (with the original portraits) was restored, the extraordinary Victorian turrets recreated and replaced on the corner towers at vast expense. Two Roman forts were revealed under the parkland turf where a golf-course had been intended. Dinefwr is open to the public along with parts of the estate and woodland as well as the medieval castle. It is a sterling achievement, worthy of the history of this remarkable place.

Smaller houses have also come into the Trust's care. In the 1980s Captain Ponsonby-Lewes offered his house and estate, Llanerchaeron in the Aeron valley, Ceredigion, to the Trust. A number of the Trust's visiting committee were apparently dismissive of the whole plan. In comparison with many Trust properties Llanerchaeron seemed small and remote. It had no special history, it was poorly furnished, it needed a great deal of restoration and had no dowry to pay for it. Why should the Trust bother? Fortunately one of the visitors saw things from another viewpoint. This, he argued, is a small but very attractive house, complete with outhouses, the home farm and estate once typical of the Welsh countryside, now very rare. When would the Trust ever be able to acquire another? He spoke with such eloquence that the Trust accepted the offer and went on to raise £5,000,000 for the restoration, in the course of which a glazier's bill was found in the attic, bearing the name of the great Welsh architect, John Nash. Today a visit to Llanerchaeron is a must for visitors to west Wales.

On the Llŷn peninsula is another such gem, even smaller than Llanerchaeron – Plas-yn-Rhiw near Aberdaron. This was rescued from near-ruin in 1939 by the three Keating sisters and restored by Clough Williams-Ellis, the most interesting and original of modern Welsh architects. Originally built in 1634, it was given a Regency makeover about 1820. It passed to the National Trust by the Keatings' bequest in 1952. Plas-yn-Rhiw doesn't present as a gentry estate home with all that that implies, but simply as a delightful Welsh haven of tranquillity. It is also unusual in that it has, thanks to the sisters, a rare feminine charm throughout. A third acquisition by the National Trust was Tŷ Mawr, Wybrnant, Penmachno, birthplace of William Morgan, translator of the Bible in Welsh, published in 1588.

Other bodies have done much for a number of Welsh houses. Aberglasney's house and garden were both derelict and overgrown before a private trust and backer brought about a phenomenal transformation. Picton Castle is the Pembrokeshire equivalent of Chirk and Powys Castle, a superbly adapted castle with a fine woodland-garden complex, once the county's political power centre. St Fagan's Castle, despite its name, is really a chateau, and is one of the great houses of south-east Wales, now part of the National Museum of Welsh Life. Plas Teg, near Mold, a fine Elizabethan house open to the public, was rescued by its owner with substantial investment, aided by Cadw but not run by them. Several historic houses which are private homes are nevertheless regularly opened by their owners: Fonmon Castle, Barry, and Gwydir Castle, Llanrwst are excellent examples; Fonmon is still owned by the family who acquired it in Cromwell's time. In the case of almost all historic houses it is wise to find out what are the dates and times of opening; many are closed during the winter, many are not open every day of the week.

A number of impressive historic houses have been restored and function as hotels. They are too numerous to name them all, but wonderfully restored Bodysgallen, near Llandudno, is certainly worth a visit. So is Nanteos, near Aberystwyth, twice rescued after approaching dereliction. Trevor Hall, Denbigh, is in superb condition and can be hired for £1,750 for a weekend! Other houses which welcome guests are Dolbelydr near Denbigh, Alltybela near Usk and Llangoed Hall in the Wye valley.

There are also several really fine town houses in Wales, and Conwy is blessed with two of them. Plas Mawr is a magnificent Elizabethan building, restored and maintained for visitors by Cadw. Even older is 14th-century Aberconwy House, owned and maintained by the National Trust. The Georgian period is represented by Llanelly House in that otherwise unlovely but interesting town and is now maintained as a heritage centre. Then there is the Judge's Lodgings at Presteigne, far more impressive than it may sound. Much more modest, but delightful, is the little property in Montgomery, surely the prettiest town in Wales, which contains the privately-run Montgomery museum.

As well as Plas Mawr, Cadw owns and runs Tretower Court, between Brecon and Crickhowell. After centuries as a gentry house it became a farm, but is now splendidly restored to its 15th-century appearance, with magnificent timber work. This is a remarkable building, complete with great hall and fine courtyard, and an ancient timber barn on the opposite side of the little road. Behind it, not easy to get at, is a hefty medieval castle keep.

There are still sad or frustrating stories. The extraordinary Sker House, standing in bleak isolation on the Glamorgan coast, was a wreck until restored in the 1990s with considerable Heritage Lottery funding. It is now in private ownership, with no encouragement for visitors. Contents of historic houses are still removed or sold by owners who can no longer afford to maintain them, especially now that there are no longer grants to help private owners maintain their homes. The loss or sale of the portraits which once looked down on their owners, reminding them of their heritage and responsibilities, is a historical disaster. Many collections have been and still are being broken up and scattered, finally disappearing into attics or emerging one by one in auction houses as 'Portrait of a Gentleman, 18th century, artist unknown'.

There were of course good paintings in Welsh houses as well the majority of run-of -the-mill pictures, and some survive. Most notable, perhaps, are the Rembrandt in the gallery at Penrhyn Castle, the Whistler mural at Plas Newydd, the Edwardian pictures in the gallery at Llangoed Hall and the truly magnificent Venetian scene by Bellotto hanging in the drawing room at Powys Castle. Some re-emerge at auction occasionally, but disappear. The Lords Dynevor and their relatives look down once more from the walls of Newton House, but alas, the Reynolds portrait of their ancestor Cecil Rice, who with her husband George Rice made Dinefwr Park what it still is, was sold a century ago by a cousin to the Frick Collection in New York. *Sic transit…*

8. Looking *for* A Welsh Muse

The medieval legend of Taliesin tells how, on the shore of Llyn Tegid – Bala Lake – the sorceress Ceridwen sought to compensate her hideous son Afagddu by giving him the gifts of knowledge and inspiration. He certainly needed help – his name means 'pitch black'. So his mother gathered herbs and roots, and set them to simmer in her cauldron for a year, stirred by her young servant Gwion. But when the drops of inspiration spurted suddenly from the cauldron and burnt Gwion's hand, he licked the wound, swallowed the drops, and became filled with all lore and learning. Although he changed his shape many times Ceridwen, as a hen, caught him in the form of a grain of wheat and swallowed him, thus becoming pregnant with a baby whom she cast to the mercy of the river Dyfi. The baby, caught in a fish-trap, was already babbling poetry when rescued, and became the poet Taliesin, infant and infinitely knowledgeable bard to Maelgwn Gwynedd, the sixth-century king of Gwynedd. Numerous surviving medieval poems were attributed to him, in which he boasts of his knowledge and his experiences throughout history.

That, brutally distilled, is the legend of Taliesin. At the heart of the legend is a real Welsh poet called Taliesin, who lived in the late sixth century and pursued his poetic craft mainly in what Welsh scholars call 'The Old North', the Welsh-speaking kingdoms of Cumbria and southern Scotland. It is likely that a handful of poems attributed to Taliesin really were written in praise of Urien, king of Rheged, and others of the warrior-chiefs of those little northern kingdoms, though the verses only survive in a late 14th-century manuscript. The later legend, and the strange poems attributed to Taliesin, is a classic example of how a man's actual career can disappear into a miasma.

Another such early poet, less celebrated in legend but equally significant for the future of Welsh poetry, was Aneirin. A 1,200-line text called 'Gododdin', or 'The Song of Aneirin', celebrates the feats and fates of a band of three hundred warriors from Gododdin, the kingdom round what is now Edinburgh, who went to do battle at Catraeth (Catterick) with the Anglo-Saxons of what is now north-east England.

> Men went to Catraeth, their host was merry,
> They drank fresh mead, but it proved poison.
> Three hundred by command in order of battle,
> And after the great shouting, there was silence.
> Though they did penance beforehand in churches,
> True the tale, death seized them.

Scholars will never be able to settle how much of the poem might derive from the seventh century, how much is later accretions. However, the work of both Aneirin and Taliesin was a major inspiration to the court poets described below; their praises were essential propaganda and encouragement for their princely patrons.

Several early Welsh poems mention a warrior called Arthur. In Welsh he is not usually given the title of 'king', but he is perceived as a fearsome fighter and voyager to the Otherworld in his ship *Prydwen*. Popular folklore of more recent times remembers him as a giant and a slayer of giants; standing stones and cromlechs are named for Arthur, commemorating his superhuman strength. The highest point of the Brecon Beacons was once known as Arthur's Seat; his buttocks would fit splendidly into the two enormous hollows on the north side of the mountain. From Wales Arthur burst fully fledged into European literature in two literary masterpieces.

One is the Latin *History of the Kings of Britain* by Geoffrey of Monmouth (*c.*1135) which tells the Arthur legend as elaborated by later French and English writers. The other is the extraordinary rip-roaring Welsh tale of *Culhwch and Olwen*, in which Arthur and a huge band of heroic, weird and grotesque characters help the young Culhwch to win the hand of Olwen, daughter of Ysbaddaden Chief Giant, with colourful exploits along the way.

Remarkably, the manuscripts of *Culhwch and Olwen* were virtually unknown either in Wales or beyond until translated and published between 1839 and 1848 by Lady Charlotte Guest, along with other Welsh medieval prose classics, as *The Mabinogion*, now available in many translations. The tales of this extraordinary collection are filled with wonders from both north and south Wales. The first four tales are called 'The Four Branches of the Mabinogi', redacted from various sources by an anonymous writer of genius. We encounter Pwyll, lord of Dyfed furiously but vainly galloping after the lovely and witty Rhiannon as her horse gently ambles away from him. Branwen, sister of Bendigeidfran, king of the Island of the Mighty, sends a starling from Ireland to let him know of her harsh treatment at the hands of the cruel Irish. But the subsequent war between the British and Irish leaves Bendigeidfran stricken, Ireland ravaged and Branwen dying of grief. Lleu Llaw Gyffes, denied by his goddess-mother the chance of marrying a woman of flesh and blood, instead marries and is betrayed by Blodeuwedd, a woman made for him from flowers. All is in limpid Welsh prose, the best ever written.

These superb stories, surviving in their present form from the late 13th century, seem in their essence to represent a Welsh imagination apparently unaltered by Norman invasion or English colonisation. However, one might well argue that the cultivated tone of courtly conversation reflects the new Cambro-Norman culture of the period. These are the peak of early Welsh achievement in prose, rising above the lower flatlands of extensive historical, religious and medical writings and translation from French and Latin texts. But the Welsh law-books, written down from the twelfth century onward, do exercise a muscular prose which deserves respect.

The twelfth-century Renaissance which did so much for European culture did not pass Wales by. Apart from the writers of stories and the law-books, an extraordinary body of poetry developed, composed and recited in praise of Welsh princes and lords. It is often extremely obscure, indeed a contemporary story-writer joked that when Arthur's poet sang his praises no-one present could understand a word. But these poets set before their patrons the ideals of courage, generosity and leadership which they were expected to emulate. Most moving of all is Gruffydd ab yr Ynad Coch's magnificent elegy on the death of Llywelyn in 1282, which reaches a truly Shakespearean climax. The poet likens the overthrow of Welsh independence to the overthrow of the world, when the sea devours the land, when the sun and stars are hurled through the skies. Chaos has prevailed.

As the English conquest finally took cultural effect, Welsh prose fell away in inspiration, but poetry adapted and survived at a high level for another three centuries. The princes were replaced as patrons by leading Welsh landowners who managed to gain office under the English Crown. Some were 'new men'; others had succeeded in preserving at least part of their patrimony. Their high descent and lineage, real or exaggerated, were to be honoured; indeed, the leading genealogists were also poets, and their craft was fundamental to the society, since a man's descent proved his entitlement to land and influence. Their work, heroic in distant origin, was grounded in that Aristotelian view of the chain of being, in which each person, and indeed all creation, acknowledges its proper place and should seek no change.

These poets of the gentry perfected the extraordinary literary fetters known as *cynghanedd*, what Gerard Manley Hopkins called 'consonantal chime', already pioneered by the poets of the heroes and princes. Although there were certainly dialects across Wales at this time, as there are today, the poets used a standard diction whether composing for patrons in Gwent or Anglesey, Clwyd or Teifiside. As well as *cynghanedd*, complex metres evolved for elevated use, while the seven-syllable couplet called the *cywydd* metre developed as by far the most utilised, with the four-line, thirty-syllable rhyming quatrain, the *englyn*, also immensely popular, both in sequence or as independent epigrams. The two measures remain popular today.

One poet above all others broke out from the conventions of praise and honour. As a gentleman Dafydd ap Gwilym was not, like most of his contemporaries and successors, dependent on patrons for his living. He knew the love-poetry of Ovid and the troubadours of Provence, and wrote not so much to describe the beauty of his female lovers as to make fun of his own passion for them which leads him into embarrassing misadventures. Above all he celebrated the month of May, the sun and the song of birds, especially the chorus which he describes as 'the woodland Mass'. Dafydd wrote with a strong awareness of contemporary European-Latin culture.

By the late 16th century traditional Welsh society was changing drastically. The abolition of Welsh law and the creation of a market in land, the expansion of trade and the political and promotional opportunities made available through the Tudor ascendancy, had all opened Wales up in a new way. Gentry often intermarried with daughters of landed English families, while Welsh heiresses were sought after by sons of the English gentry. Sons were sent to English schools, then to Oxford or the Inns of Court. Patronage of the poets declined, while the rich Catholic fabric of life – abbey and chantry, rood-screen and pilgrim shrine, often praised by the poets – had been torn down and swept away by the Reformation.

At this critical moment the need to enlighten the supposed superstitious ignorance of the common people lit a new fire in the apparently dying furnace of the Welsh language. Since the mass of people were monoglot Welsh-speakers, translations of the Bible and Book of Common Prayer were clearly necessary to satisfy the ideals of the Protestant Reformation. This was commanded by Act of Parliament in 1563, thus giving the Welsh language a new status. Thanks to a handful of great Welsh scholars, a new life began for the ancient tongue. Early efforts at translation were too Latinate, but William Morgan, using much of the language of the classical poets, created what was virtually a new, dignified, rich and powerful prose style for the Bible which, despite later and more contemporary versions, is still revered today and, like the English King James Bible, provides a host of phrases in everyday use.

The decline and disappearance of patronage did not mean the end of traditional Welsh poetry. *Beirdd gwlad* (poets of the countryside) continue to the present day to write on a social level about matters of concern to them and to their neighbours. They and others also wrote extensively in free measures (rhyme and metre but no *cynghanedd*) in praise of all kinds of subjects, usually calling their poems 'carols'.

Rather like English literature in the 15th century, Welsh literature went through a long period without any great inspiration. Prose was virtually all religious, often translated from English. At first, work was printed in London, but after government regulations were relaxed, printing presses moved to Shrewsbury after 1694 and to Wales in 1718. Almanacs and ballads became increasingly popular.

A small coterie of men who delighted in Welsh learning and scholarship transformed the course of literature between 1750 and 1810. Major pioneering efforts were made to publish masterpieces of earlier Welsh poetry and a great deal of Welsh prose, including the Welsh law and history texts, but the *Mabinogion* tales were inexplicably ignored. The *eisteddfod* was revived (see chapter 10); the classical metres were rejuvenated, especially by Goronwy Owen. Pioneer efforts were made to publish magazines in Welsh. There was a great widening of literacy, but the aim of composition was still to achieve the salvation of souls, and some of the best poetry appeared as hymns by William Williams, Pantycelyn; Morgan Rhys and others.

Gradually during the 19th century Welsh weekly, monthly and quarterly periodicals began to be published. Small increases in people's available spending money brought a huge efflorescence of publishing, with a printer in almost every Welsh town. Edinburgh publishers sold large quantities of Welsh Bibles and other classics, while the major Welsh printer-publisher Thomas Gee sponsored a ten-volume encyclopaedia which sold out, making a second edition necessary. Unfortunately, in retrospect, the vast body of Welsh publishing was religious. Even this great *Gwyddoniadur* began every entry with a note on what the Bible has to say on almost any subject. Most Welsh writers were unwilling to meet the challenge of the new geology and of Darwinism. From 1868 the National Eisteddfod's poetry competitions for the Chair and Crown offered an annual summit of achievement not matched by inspiration, though fortunately this would change.

Despite much success, linguistic decline was in the offing. From 1870 children were subjected to compulsory teaching through English, with the support of their mostly monoglot parents. A generation grew up not knowing that their teachers could speak Welsh. Although the number of Welsh-speakers continued to increase until 1911, the number of English-speakers grew faster. Popular English publications, especially newspapers and magazines, pushed their way into the Welsh market, covering a much wider range of subject-matter.

Paradoxically, the actual standard of Welsh writing began to improve under the pressure of better education, particularly through the University Colleges of Wales. Prejudice against fiction and drama declined, and the first major Welsh novelist, Daniel Owen (d. 1895), entertained tens of thousands of readers. New and exciting poets appeared: T. Gwynn Jones, Robert Williams Parry, Thomas Parry-Williams. After World War I, the short story flourished in Welsh literary periodicals, reaching a peak in the work of Kate Roberts. Welsh literary criticism and poetic drama were created almost single-handed by the virtuoso Saunders Lewis.

This renaissance of Welsh literature was achieved in spite of severe difficulties. Most publishing was still done by jobbing printers as a sideline. Welsh bookshops were scarce. The financial rewards for both printer and writer were minimal. From the 1960s, however, increasing government grants for Welsh publishing through the Welsh Books Council, and the opening of a remarkable number of independent Welsh bookshops, have made publishing Welsh literature easier than it ever was, while writers gain some reward for their work. But the world never stops changing. Much of the available talent in Welsh writing is now swallowed up by profitable scriptwriting for Welsh television, leaving Ceridwen's cauldron rather less bubbly than it has been. But shrinking budgets threaten this source of inspiration.

9. Looking *for* Welsh Names

I can hear the reader sigh – Welsh names are so boring! Everybody's called Jones, Hughes, Roberts, Davies, Williams or Jenkins. But let's pause for a moment. What do the English cricketer Graham Gooch and the Welsh rugby international Ian Gough, not to mention the English Puritan Thomas Gouge, have in common? They each have the same Welsh surname, originally *Goch*, meaning red-headed. John Badham the film director, the linguistic scholar Oliver Onions, the scriptwriter Peter Devonald and the Victorian poet Thomas Love Beddoes all have Welsh names. Badham is from *ab Adam* (son of Adam), Onions from Welsh *Einion*, Devonald from *Dyfnwal* and Beddoes from *Bedo*, an affectionate form of Maredudd, believe it or not. Thomas Dewey the American philosopher and Melvil Dewey, inventor of the library cataloguing system named after him, derive their surname from *Dewi*, the oldest Welsh form of the name David. That should be enough to dismiss fears that the subject is necessarily dull.

Of course the names Jones, Evans, Hughes, Roberts, Davies, Williams or Jenkins (which we might crudely collectivise as Jones *et al.*) are indeed extremely common. Some readers may remember an incident years ago when a Welsh male voice choir went to sing in communist East Germany. So many passports were in the name of Jones that the border officials became suspicious and held up proceedings while they demanded an explanation. Obviously they thought the hoary joke about Jones the Spy was true. But this chapter will show that there is a great deal of variety in Welsh surnames – especially in England.

As for those common names, Jones *et al.,* each obviously derives from a common male given name – John, Evan, Hugh, Robert, David, William, Jenkin. Those names are all part of a common west European stock; not one of them is an English name, though they have been adapted for English use. In the Welsh versions, each given name has had the English possessive *–'s* added, in the same way that the English added –son to the same names, thus Johnson, Davidson, Williamson, Jenkinson, Thomson. So if that set of surnames, Jones *et al.,* are Welsh by adoption but not by origin, how did they come to be so common in Wales?

First we may well ask, why surnames at all? – a question to which there are several answers. The first surnames in Wales and England were simply nicknames added to a given name in order to distinguish between individuals. These names could derive from a personal characteristic (e.g. hair colour), one's place of origin, one's employment in life, or lastly the name of a parent (usually but not always the father's name). The men who really gave status to surnames were the aristocratic Norman invaders, who usually used their place of origin in France, and these could become hereditary, as in the case of the de Clare family, lords of Glamorgan and of great estates elsewhere. (The French *de* simply meant 'from, of', but became a sign of an aristocratic family.)

By the 13th century the English crown was taxing large numbers of people, who had to be listed by their first names and identifiers, and by the 14th century at the latest these identifying names were nearly always hereditary. Of course a man could deliberately change his name, as when a Welsh Williams family moved to Huntingdonshire and changed their name to Cromwell. A change of spelling might suffice, as in the case of the great family of the Marquises of Salisbury, whose family name is Cecil, altered from their original Welsh name *Seisyllt* for easier pronunciation and recognition.

With some exceptions, the Welsh were content to develop the use of patronymics or fathers' names as identifiers. This gave the common formula *n* + *ap* + *n*, e.g. Dafydd ap Gwilym. For women it was *n* + *ach* + *n*, e.g. Marged ach Ifan. Obviously *ap* and *ach* mean 'son' and 'daughter' respectively. But this is not a family-name system as we know it today, since the son of Dafydd ap Gwilym (if he'd had one) might have been given his grandfather's baptismal name, e.g. Gwilym ap Dafydd, or another name altogether, e.g. Llywelyn ap Dafydd. This formala persisted in Wales for the vast majority of the population until the early 18th century, and clung on in rural fastnesses into the early 19th century. It is a nightmare for genealogists, especially as the popular stock of Welsh given names shrank rapidly from the 15th century onwards. Parish and other records show that even though the *ap* form was not acceptable for official purposes and the –'s usage replaced it, so that Dafydd ap Gwilym became David Williams, his son might still be called William Davies. An additional complication for genealogists is that well into the 18th-century women in Welsh rural society did not change their names on marriage.

Male given names which were originally Welsh did not need changing, though they sometimes had to metamorphose. Morgan was unchangeable, though some families would casually add an 's to conform with common practice. Rhys did not need to change, but was often anglicised as Rees, Rice or Reece. Owain became Owen, Ieuan and Ifan became Evan, while Llywelyn was reshaped, under the influence of Welsh *llew* (a lion) and internal repetition, to Llewellyn, and Gruffudd to Griffith.

The Great Welsh Name Change of the 16th to the 18th

centuries offered an alternative to adopting the form in –'s. If a paternal name began with a vowel, an *H–* or an *Rh–*, it was perfectly possible for the *ap* to be swallowed into the name; so ab Evan became Bevan, ap Owen became Bowen. From *H–* and *P–* names came a whole series: Powell, Pugh, Parry, Penry, Prytherch, Pritchard, Preece, Price, Probert, Powell, Pumphrey, Popkin.

Some patronymics of Welsh origin are not so easily recognised, as in the case of Onions/Einion quoted above. *Day* is quite a common English surname, and the majority of people of that name may not realise that it comes from Welsh *Dai*, the well-known familiar form of David. At least some English people surnamed Welling and Wellen might be surprised to know that their names are abbreviated from *Llywelyn*, a name which has produced other abbreviated forms such as Lellow. The length of the name, and the difficulty presented by the initial *Ll–* to the English, meant that many Welshmen were encouraged to adopt the name *Lewis* as an alternative, thus explaining the frequency of Lewis as a surname in Wales. Pronunciation difficulties also explain how Maredudd became Meredith, though not that it has now become a girl's name.

The overwhelming use of the patronymic system meant that other kinds of surname are scarce in Wales. English has numerous examples of all the other classes of surname. English people have a host of occupational surnames, from Archer, Baker and Butcher to Smith, Thatcher and Wainwright. Welsh has only the long-established *Saer*, a carpenter or craftsman. English has a riot of surnames from nicknames, from the commonplace Black, Grey and White to exotics like Smellie and Gotobed (both genuine). Welsh has a few such names: Gwyn (English – fair), Dee (from *Du* = black), Donne (from *Dwn* = brown, in its turn a loan word from English *dun*),

Lloyd, Floyd and Flood (all from *Llwyd* = grey), Clough (from *Cloff* = lame), Dew (from *Tew* = fat).

Places and individual place-names provided a vast number of English surnames, whether one thinks in terms of Field, Hill and Green or particular placenames such as Churchill, Washington and York. Wales has produced its share: Barry (as a surname), Cardiff, Conway, Denby (Welsh – *Dinbych*, English – *Denbigh*), Glynne (*glyn* = a steep-sided valley), and less obviously Carew, Scourfield and Prendergast (all Pembrokeshire place-names), Pennant, Yale and Gwinnett (from *Gwynedd*). Elihu Yale, founder of the American university, was from the Welsh district of Yale (Welsh – *Iâl*), while Welshman Button Gwinnett was a signer of the American Declaration of Independence. The name *Dolben* is a puzzle; the only reliable scholarly work on Welsh surnames doesn't mention it, but it is still in use both in Wales and beyond. It might derive from Dolbenmaen, near Porthmadog in Gwynedd.

The surname *Vaughan* deserves comment. The present English pronunciation ('Vawn') is reminiscent of the problems English speakers had with French and other names like Beauchamp (pronounced Beecham) and Cholmondley (Chumley). *Vaughan* is the Welsh word *Bychan* (small, young), which when used as a nickname changed its initial letter in a way familiar to anyone who has struggled to learn Welsh. *Fychan* was used when a boy was baptized with his father's own baptismal name, so Dafydd ap Dafydd would be known simply as Dafydd Fychan, i.e. Young Dafydd or David. In time it became the surname of several well-known Welsh families: the Vaughans of Corsygedol, of Trawsgoed, of Courtfield. They are not related to one another.

Just as Hebrew contributed more place-names in Wales than to any other country in Europe, so it gave the Welsh a few surnames. I know of no study of these names in a Welsh context, but they are there: Aaron, Elias, Emanuel, Joel and Habbakuk. These names probably derive from the period of religious revivals in the Wales of 1730–1870.

Genealogists of the future will certainly endure an additional Welsh frustration to those already outlined. Deliberately changing one's surname has become a practice with a minority in Wales, particularly those afflicted, as they see it, with one of the really common Welsh surnames, especially Jones. Various ways of achieving this end have been developed. The *ap* form was revived a century ago and is still used, but hasn't really take root. More popular has been to give a child a distinctive middle name, often derived from a place of personal significance to one or both parents. Thus we have the contemporary sculptor John Meirion Jones, easily distinguished in discussion of his work by simply referring to him as John Meirion. In 1920s Wales a writer of drama and light fiction called John Ellis Williams became popular. When a young and promising scholar of the same name began to come to prominence, he adopted a local place-name and became John Ellis Caerwyn Williams, known in conversation simply as Caerwyn. A further development has been simply to drop the paternal surname altogether, either using the father's middle name as a surname or adopting a new name altogether.

This willingness to change one's name for the sake of recognition certainly goes back to the 18th century, when the great polymath Lewis Morris became known among his circle as Llywelyn Du o Fôn, an interesting example of reverting from Lewis to Llywelyn. Adopting a nom de plume became a popular custom followed by many writers. Among the earliest was the fine Welsh lyric poet Alun (1797–1840). He clearly preferred a more Welsh way of identifying himself (from the river Alun near his home) rather than his birth-name of John Blackwell, much too English a name for a Welsh poet. Thus 'Alun' became a popular boy's name in Wales, unrelated to the Breton 'Alan', which has been borrowed into English through French 'Alain'.

Use of a place-name often distinguishes individual writers. Some poets of the 16th and 17th centuries had place-names as identifiers, thus Wiliam Cynwal and the brothers Rhys and Siôn Cain. The greatest of the hymn-writers, William Williams (1717–91) never referred to his birthplace on his many title-pages, but the elegies published on his death certainly did so, and till this day he is simply 'Pantycelyn'. Indeed, there were many other William Williamses publishing between 1740 and 1860, identifiable individually as William Williams Llandygái, Williams o'r Wern, Gwilym Twrog, Gwilym Peris, Gwilym ab Iorwerth, Gwilym ab Ioan, Gwilym Cyfeiliog, Carw Coch, Creuddynfab, Y Lefiad, Myfyr Wyn, Caledfryn and his son Ap Caledfryn (the latter an artist rather than a writer). Each one was originally a William Williams!

Some bardic names seem quite eccentric today. Perhaps the now-forgotten Robert Owen (1803–70) was so uncomfortably aware of his lack of genius that he inflated his ego by calling himself Eryron Gwyllt Gwalia ('Wild Eagles of Wales'). Other extraordinary noms-de-plume include Index, Brutus, Tau Gimel, Vulcan and Minimus. The long-forgotten but once notorious Caernarfon antiquarian William Owen (1785–1864) was nicknamed *Y Pâb* (The Pope), because he defended Catholic emancipation, and was much loathed for doing so. At least Robert Williams (1830–77) had a sense of humour, choosing the penname Trebor Mai – try reading it backwards. That artificial name Trebor was soon adopted as a given name for boys. Another Robert, Robert Ambrose

Jones (1848–1906), the finest Welsh prose stylist of his age, rechristened himself by turning the Ambrose and Jones in his name back into Welsh as Emrys ap Iwan.

The practice of name-changing continued through the 20th century. Thus, for Welsh eisteddfod-goers the name of Cynan is revered; he was a fine popular poet as well as master and reformer of organisation and ceremonies at the National Eisteddfod. He wasn't at all well-known by his registered name of Albert Evans-Jones (1895–1970). Similarly, the outstanding poet David James Jones (1899–1968) took the name of Alltwen, his Swansea-valley birthplace, reversed it and became Gwenallt. His widow is always referred to as 'Mrs Gwenallt' and their daughter's name is simply Mair Gwenallt.

Cynan and Gwenallt were only two of a number of significant figures in recent Welsh history who are better-known by their adopted names than their names of registration. The name *Mabon* immediately summons up the bearded, portly figure of William Abraham (1842–1922) a major figure in Welsh industrial history and the first coalminer elected to parliament. John Williams (1811–62) is not a name that springs directly to the mind of anyone interested in the Victorian revival of the National Eisteddfod, but as Ab Ithel, he is a significant figure in Welsh culture, despite his suspect scholarship.

Modern Welsh nicknames like Mock the Milk, Dai Double Yolk (father of twins), Twm Eggs and Jones the Spy (only joking, that one) are not as lively or varied as they used to be. My father could reel off a list of nicknames of people in his home village of Pontardawe, some of them quite obscene. Farmers may still refer to each other simply by the names of their farms, and priests to each other by the names of their parishes.

It will be justly complained that only passing reference has been made to women's surnames. This inevitably reflects the patriarchal nature of European society in general and Wales in particular. However, Welsh female names were occasionally given to a boy as an identifier, especially if illegitimate. Quite the most famous example is that of Thomas Jones of Fountain Gate (d. 1607), always known in Welsh as Twm Siôn Cati. He was the illegitimate son of his mother Catherine, of which Cati is an affectionate form still in use. One influential Welsh female name is Angharad, anglicised especially in Pembrokeshire and the Marches to Ancret, giving a surname which occurs often in Shropshire records, sometimes as Ankaret, which might mislead the suspicious to think that a holy anchorite had once lapsed into fatherhood.

Women writers, like men, have adopted pen names. Sarah Edith Wynne (1842–97) became Eos Cymru, the Welsh nightingale. Since there were many male poets who took Eos as the first part of their noms-de-plume, her choice did not betray her gender. The novelist Anne Adelisa Puddicombe (1836–1908), although writing in English, chose to conceal her work under the masculine name Allen Raine, thus following a well-known fashion among English women authors. The historian Jane Williams (1806–85) adopted the genderless 'Ysgafell', apparently meaning 'prey, booty', a choice which I do not understand. Sarah Jane Rees (1839–1916), poet, editor and teacher of navigation, derived the name Cranogwen from her village home, Llangrannog. The '-wen' ending makes it clear that she was a woman and obviously proud of it. In recent years a number of female media performers and writers have abandoned their patronymics for more colourful names: thus Siân Cothi, Heulwen Haf ('Summer Sunshine'), Heledd Cynwal, Bethan Gwanas.

A particular feature of Welsh women's names is the way in which the stock of names considered usable actually dwindled quite dramatically in the later medieval period. There had been plenty of medieval women's names; to give a list here would be otiose, but it would include Nest, Non, Mair, Gwerful, Morfydd, Lleucu, Angharad, Gwladus and Gwenhwyfar. By the 16th century Catrin/Catherine and Marged/Margaret had become immensely popular while Welsh names were in decline, and by the early 18th century there were hardly any Welsh female names in use – certainly not in common use. Elizabeth, Catherine, Margaret, Susanna, Sage, Eleanor, Joan and Bridget certainly outnumber the few surviving examples of names like Golau (Welsh – *light*), Gaenor (from Gwenhwyfar) and Gwen (from Gwenllïan). The French form *Guinevere* is a rare example of an original Welsh name rendered into another language through literary borrowing. The Welsh original was popular in medieval Wales, since it didn't have the strong connotation of adultery which attached to Guinevere in the French tales of Arthur. The English adopted their own form of the Welsh original – Jennifer.

During the second half of the 19th century the national revival in Welsh culture saw the adoption both of early names like Gwladus and the invention of new ones like Dilys ('faultless'), a process which has continued to the present day. There was also the practice of inventing or reviving Welsh versions of English names, thus Jane > Siân, Janet > Sioned, Elizabeth > Bethan or Betsan, Margaret > Marged. The termination -wen, suggesting Welsh *gwen*, the feminine form of *gwyn* meaning 'fair', gives Anwen. The root *car-* ('love') gives Cerys, Carys and Carwen, while flower and other natural names produce Ffion ('foxglove'), Eirlys ('snowdrop'), Seren ('star') and Eira ('snow'). Tegwen is simply 'beautiful', while Rhiannon and Branwen (with Bronwen) derive from literary legends, as do Esyllt and Enid.

An interesting revival is that of the name Siwan. The first Siwan was Joan (d. 1237), daughter of King John and wife of Llywelyn the Great, whom we have already encountered. The name was popularised because Siwan is the titular heroine of the finest drama in Welsh, by Saunders Lewis. On the other hand I know of no woman or girl called after Saunders Lewis's other play titled for its heroine – Blodeuwedd. This is hardly surprising. The original Blodeuwedd was created by two wizards from flowers (Blodeuwedd = flower-face) as a wife for the hero Lleu Llaw Gyffes, since he was magically prevented from marrying a woman of flesh and blood. Alas, Blodeuwedd was unfaithful to her husband, and was turned into an owl by her creators – not a fate to wish on a baby girl. On the other hand, the alarming story of the sorceress Ceridwen, mother of the poet Taliesin, already met above, has not hindered parents from its use. She is, after all, the origin of poetic inspiration.

It is much to be wished that scholars would give time to the further investigation of Welsh personal names. The popular booklets for choosing names for Welsh babies are not at all reliable. To give a single example, the name Enid, correctly pronounced with a short 'e' like Emily and Eleanor, is *not* derived from the Welsh *enaid* meaning 'soul'. The best explanation is that it was originally a Breton name, woven into French-Welsh-English Arthurian legend in the 12th and 13th centuries and popularised by Tennyson's 'Idylls of the King'; he knew his *Mabinogion*.

Having spent so much time on surnames in general and on female baptismal names, justice insists on at least some minimal attention to male baptismal names. Prior to the Norman invasions the vast majority of Welsh names were either rooted in Celtic, derived from the Bible or borrowed from Latin. The names of Celtic (British) origin are typified by such names as Rhys ('ardour'), Morgan ('sea-coast dweller'), Hywel ('easily-seen, tall'). The Bible yielded several early names, especially Dewi and Dafydd as forms of David, and of Ieuan, Ioan, Ifan as equivalents of John. The saints' names Padarn and Rhystud are certainly of Latin origin, while Owain/Owen has the modern equivalent Eugene, meaning 'well-born'.

A few early English names penetrated Welsh culture; the princely name Uchdryd has the rare English equivalent Oughtred, and Edwin was also gathered in to become a Welsh name. Later English names were also adopted: Watkin, Jenkin, Hopkin. The Norman barons contributed several names which were to become immensely popular: Robert, Hugh, William. The later passion for choral music bestowed the names Haydn and Handel on many sons of Valley choristers – but whence the popularity of Byron as a given name in Wales is beyond me. And with that, *digon yw digon* – enough is enough.

10. Looking *for* The Land of Song

'Praise the Lord, we are a musical nation,' says the Reverend Eli Jenkins in Dylan Thomas's *Under Milk Wood*. It's one of the most quoted lines by any Welsh writer, cited more often in irony than in straight appreciation. What does the Reverend mean? What did Dylan Thomas mean? What do the quoters mean? The vicar of Llaregyb is of course responding to Polly Garter's Rabelaisian song, 'Tom, Dick and Harry were three fine men'. Irony or innocence is in the voice of the actor and the ear of the hearer; either interpretation or both are legitimate. Whether or not Eli Jenkins is ironic, Dylan Thomas certainly is, poking gentle fun at the cliché of Wales as the Land of Song, the belief that every Welsh person (especially every Welsh *man*) was born a singer. That belief is of course nonsense. People's ability to sing depends on the culture and tradition of their time and place rather than on the individual's larynx, let alone any pseudo-racial characteristic. Virtually everyone can sing, but not everyone knows how. However, music is certainly an important part of what might be called 'the culture of Welshness'.

There is an enormous variety of Welsh music available: in live performances, on TV, radio, records and the internet. At one end of the spectrum are the BBC National Symphony Orchestra of Wales and the Welsh National Opera Company, to both of which Wales owes a huge debt. There are numerous choirs, large and small, regional amateur orchestras and the Mid Wales Opera group. There are fine brass and silver bands to be heard, offspring of a long tradition, especially in industrial Wales both north and south. There are rock and folk-groups; there are specialised styles of singing, *Cerdd Dant* and *Plygain*. The former involves a soloist or group who sing, to put it crudely, one tune to the accompaniment of another. Almost extinct by 1900, it has been vigorously revived, and can be heard at youth and national eisteddfodau and at the annual festival of Cerdd Dant in late autumn. *Plygain* is a particular form of Christmas carol service, where a wide range of unaccompanied traditional Welsh carols are sung by family groups, small parties and soloists. It is enjoying a new vogue in and beyond its Powys heartland.

The growing Nonconformity of 18th and especially 19th century Wales placed great emphasis on congregational hymn-singing. By the 1830s many music societies had been formed across Wales and a good knowledge of a limited number of musical forms developed. The intensity of Welsh chapel culture, especially in the tightly-knit communities of the industrial areas in both north and south Wales, gave every opportunity for choral singing to flourish. It was hugely encouraged by the tonic sol-fa movement. Sol-fa uses letters to represent musical pitch, which made it far cheaper to print music than by using the expensive engraving method then necessary for printing music in traditional staff notation. Singing in four-part harmony was easy to teach and scores became cheap to buy and easy to learn.

Chapels developed their own annual singing festivals and many communities had eisteddfodau. Choirs used chapel facilities for rehearsal and performance, and a culture of competition, especially between male voice choirs from about 1860, grew wondrously. The skills and personalities of rival conductors were absorbing topics of comment and discussion. Mixed choirs took readily to singing classical oratorios by Haydn, Mendelssohn and others.

The classical repertory for male choirs, 'the sound of Wales', was largely limited to hymns, choruses and to specially composed works, but this did not prevent them developing a considerable range of material. The speciality of these male choirs is a rich velvety tone, running dramatically from pianissimo to fortissimo and back again. The zenith of Welsh choral singing came with the victories at the Crystal Palace in 1872 and 1873 of the South Wales Choral Union, over 450 strong, under their conductor Caradog (Griffith Rhys Jones). Welsh male choirs toured America; indeed, in 1908/9 the Treorchy Choir toured the world. Eisteddfod contests between the great choirs electrified audiences into the 1960s, but then many choirs gave up competing to concentrate on recording and concert work, and on broadening their repertoire, which had become too narrow. However, good choral singing, especially by young choirs, can still be heard at eisteddfodau and concerts.

Impoverishment of the chapel culture after 1960 and the growth of television, home central heating and other distractions have reduced the number of major choirs and increased the average age of their members. Schools largely failed to replace the chapels in the teaching choral singing. Instead, from the 1940s the school emphasis was far more on instrumental music. However the

Welsh musical culture received a huge fillip in 1947 with the establishment of the International Eisteddfod at Llangollen. Originating with the work of a British Council officer, Harold Tudor, the eisteddfod was long associated with the Welsh musical scholar and publisher W.S. Gwynn Williams. The eisteddfod draws competitors in music and dance from all over the world, and many of the world's greatest soloists have sung in its concerts.

Eisteddfod, both National and National Youth, did much to encourage solo singers. Throughout the 20th century Wales produced a string of great opera and concert performers: Sir Geraint Evans, Sir Stuart Burrows, Bryn Terfel, Dame Margaret Price, Elizabeth Vaughan, Dennis O'Neill and many more.

Welsh choirs can be heard in television competitions, where the best Welsh choirs still excel. The heartlands of choral singing are still the Valleys and the former industrial areas of the north, not popular with tourists who would like to hear choral singing. However, choirs such as Llanelli, Treorchy, Dunvant, Rhosllanerchrugog, Trelawnyd, Bridgend, the Morriston Orpheus and the Brythoniaid (Blaenau Ffestiniog) all have websites giving performance dates. They and others have recorded their work, admirable souvenirs of Wales for visitors. There is too a rapidly growing movement of smaller, younger choirs outside the choral heartlands, such as Ysgol Glanaethwy and the remarkable Only Men Aloud and its offspring, Only Boys Aloud, which have brought a distinct razzmatazz to the concert platform.

The school emphasis on instrumental music has certainly borne fruit, though arguably at the expense of singing. Schools and counties formed orchestras, culminating in the National Youth Orchestra of Wales, which has for many years reached a really high standard and played a wide variety of classical music at the National Eisteddfod and on tour every August. The pioneer classical composer in Wales was undoubtedly Joseph Parry (1841–1903), now mainly remembered for his wonderful hymn-tune 'Aberystwyth' and his opera, *Hywel and Blodwen*. He was followed by a number of talented men and women whose music is still played: Morfydd Llwyn Owen, David de Lloyd, Meirion Williams, Grace Williams, Daniel Jones, Alun Hoddinott and William Mathias, to name only the dead. The harpist Osian Ellis was perhaps the first Welsh instrumentalist to achieve international renown; today pianist Llŷr Williams and harpist Catrin Finch bid fair to rival him.

Whereas Nonconformity virtually created the Welsh tradition of choral music, it nearly killed off Welsh traditional music. Tradition-bearers became ashamed of the songs they knew because of their secular nature and connection with tavern culture. Nevertheless, a rich variety of songs were saved by collectors, and numbers like 'The Ash-Grove' and 'All Through the Night', after polishing up by Victorian arrangers and translators, became part of the general repertoire of British songbooks, along with 'The Bonnie Banks o' Loch Lomond', 'Cockles and Mussels', 'Widdecombe Fair' and so on. Others were really harp melodies to which Victorian versifiers gave words. Yet others derived from particular festivals, whether religious or more primitive, like the New Year wren-hunting and Mari Lwyd rituals. Others belonged to the 'stable-loft' tradition, while many are love songs. Some folk songs are typified by comical exaggeration, others by the macaronic use of English phrases mixed with Welsh. At the same time a vigorous tradition of English folk singing was maintained in the Gower peninsula, most famously by Phil Tanner (d. 1952). Today there are plenty of recordings of Welsh folk song and instrumental music by soloists and groups, and there are competitions in eisteddfodau.

The instrument most associated with Wales is the harp, though there is nothing especially Welsh about the harp's origins. However the traditional triple harp, made entirely of wood and with three rows of strings, survived longer in Wales than anywhere else because it was cheap and light; the pedal or concert harp by contrast is expensive and heavy. Early Welsh harpers, often blind, played the triple harp with great success in London and elsewhere, but in Victorian times the concert harp was adopted, especially by the Welsh Romany musician John Roberts, who with his nine sons formed a remarkable harp-choir. By the 1950s only one musician remained who played the triple harp, Nansi Richards (1888–1979). Fortunately her example and teaching revived the instrument and its attractive tone; triple harps are once again made and played in Wales.

Well into the 20th century Welsh music remained almost entirely in the classical-choral-folk modes. The culture of the English music hall had little influence, and American syncopation was unknown until the 1940s, when a three-strong close-harmony group of talented Bangor students, Triawd y Coleg, became enormously popular on the radio with a number of fresh and comic songs. They performed alongside the rumbustuous figure of Bob Tai'r Felin, who had his own repertoire of characteristically vigorous songs which became popular with Welsh-speakers.

Only with the advent of television did Welsh audiences begin to hear Welsh-language pop-singing of the kind familiar for decades elsewhere. English skiffle-groups had become popular and influential, generating many Welsh imitators; by the late '60s there were Welsh groups and soloists galore, many recording with a Welsh company, Sain. Rock and reggae underlay the attractive work of, respectively, Meic Stevens and Geraint Jarman and their groups. Protest and patriotism, brilliantly projected, gave Dafydd Iwan decades of success with a range of satirical and patriotic ballads. The National Eisteddfod gave rockers and poppers a stage as far away from the main pavilion as possible.

Some Welsh popular musicians looked for a wider audience than Wales. Donald Peers from Ammanford vocally seduced

1940s Englishwomen with his tenor charm, then Mary Hopkins briefly enchanted the world in the 1960s. Tom Jones took Las Vegas by storm, while Shirley Bassey went worldwide with 'Goldfinger'. Finally Welsh groups made a wider breakthrough, especially the Manic Street Preachers, Stereophonics and Catatonia. English students danced to the voice of Cerys Matthews singing 'Every day when I wake up I thank the Lord I'm Welsh'.

It's true that at the height of the tourist season in August there's little live Welsh music to be heard outside the National Eisteddfod. But there's no doubt that Welsh music is alive and throbbing. The internet is full of information, and not only from choir, group and band websites. In popular terms especially, musical Wales of 1950 was a cultural semi-desert compared to today.

11. Looking *for* Welsh Sport

Looking for sport in Wales means getting used to some strange contradictions with which outsiders love to tease us. 'Shouldn't the great Ryan Giggs have had a chance to play in the World Cup finals for a British team? What about Gareth Bale?' 'What are Swansea and Cardiff doing in the English Premier League? You've got a league of your own!' 'Isn't it strange that outstanding Welsh cricketers – and there have been a few – play for England?' 'Why did rugby, that archetypal English public-school game, prove so popular with Welsh industrial workers?' 'Isn't it odd that Welsh athletes represent Wales in the Commonwealth Games but the United Kingdom in the Olympics?'

Some football fans, especially outside Britain, wax indignant about the anomalies of their sport as organised in the United Kingdom. Because England, Wales, Northern Ireland and Scotland have their own independent Football Associations, they have always played as separate entities in all international competitions. The consequent foreign accusation is that the United Kingdom, which is one state, gets four bites at the cherry where other states only get one each. Some British enthusiasts complain to the contrary; if the UK fielded one football team it would contain the cream of all four countries, mostly English but strengthened at various times by exceptional Welsh players like John Charles, Ivor Allchurch, Ian Rush and Ryan Giggs, not to mention Scots and Irish stars. But don't suggest the idea in the hearing of the Football Association of Wales (FAW), the third oldest FA in the world, founded in 1876. The FAW is a permanent member of the Federation of International

> The FAW constitution was drawn up at a long Saturday evening meeting in the Wynnstay Arms, Ruabon, in 1876. When a zealous policeman sought to stop the session, since the hotel should have closed, Sir Watkin Williams-Wynn, MP, JP, went next door, pronounced the magistrates' court open and extended the hotel's opening hours so that the task could be completed. Only in Wales...

Football Associations, and has no desire to be downgraded. Nor would Scotland's Tartan Army be pleased, to say the least, by such a plan.

Despite its separate identity, Welsh football is extremely close to English football. In the past Wales had six football clubs in the major English Leagues, but only Cardiff City (founded 1899) and Swansea City (founded 1912) have been in the Leagues in recent years. From autumn 2013 the two clubs will both be in the Premier League, joined in the Second Division by Newport County. Former League club Wrexham plays in the English Conference League, but has aspirations. Most Welsh international stars play for clubs in England. Wales has its own leagues; winners of the Welsh Premier League and the Welsh FA Cup play in the early rounds of European competitions. Occasionally such minnows bring off exceptional victories, as in 1962 when Bangor City defeated Napoli 2–0. At the time of writing Swansea City is doing well in the Europa League.

Recent years have seen both football and rugby clubs moving to new grounds. Cardiff City play at the Cardiff City stadium, while Swansea City and the Ospreys play at the Liberty stadium, Swansea. Hallowed grounds like the Vetch and Stradey Park are no more. International football games are usually played at the Cardiff City or Millennium stadia.

Football is surely played by more men and women in Wales than any other sport, but rugby draws larger crowds for international matches, and is generally counted as the national game. The most obvious reason for this status is that rugby is the only game in which Wales plays regularly against the world's top teams with the expectation (or reasonable hope) of winning. Subsequent pressure on rugby players and coaches is enormous. Graham Henry, the first New Zealander to coach the national XV, memorably claimed that 'New Zealanders are fanatical about rugby. The Welsh are hysterical!'

Rugby in Wales has an odd history. It certainly owed its origin to Welshmen from Oxbridge and English public schools, and the first ever team in Wales, in 1850, represented St David's College, Lampeter – all the players were candidates for Church priesthood if not already ordained. However, once the game had taken root in Swansea (the first club, founded in 1870), followed by Cardiff, Newport and Llanelli, it not only flourished but spread quickly into the industrial valleys. The first international was played against England in 1881, when Wales were heavily defeated.

Quickly Wales rose to compete with the best. Between 1900 and 1914 they defeated all the home nations in one season six times, claiming the Triple Crown each time, and also beat the otherwise all-victorious New

Unlike football, United Kingdom teams in rugby (Lions), cricket, hockey and athletics operate a dual international policy. Where UK teams exist, Welsh players can be chosen, but there are also regular competitions in which Welsh national teams appear. Cricket is different in that only very rarely does a team represent Wales. In the 1920s, a Wales XI beat the West Indies touring team. In the first serious Wales-England match, in 2002, Wales triumphed.

Zealand tourists in 1905. Great War mortality and the post-war economic catastrophe severely weakened Welsh rugby, worsened by the departure of many talented players to professional rugby league. Welsh rugby authorities turned a blind eye to their clubs making payments to players ('boot money'), but any player taking even an unpaid trial for a League club risked a lifelong ban from the Union game if identified. As with football, there was a steep decline in club support because the unemployed could not afford to pay to watch matches.

However, the period saw the strengthening of rugby in Welsh boys' grammar schools, which regularly fielded formidable teams in fair but ferocious competition. Clubs were founded in north Wales. The 1930s saw international victory at Twickenham and another triumph over the New Zealanders. Even more remarkable was the defeat of the New Zealanders by the Swansea club, who fielded two brilliant schoolboys at half-back, Claude Davey and Haydn Tanner. Of such stuff is legend created. Cardiff, Llanelli and Newport can also boast of past successes against one or more touring teams from New Zealand, Australia and South Africa.

After WWII Welsh club rugby rose to new heights, competing in an informal 'national league' of Wales, and regularly defeating the finest English clubs. Internationally Wales experienced mixed fortunes, while managing to defeat the New Zealand All Blacks for the third and (hitherto, last) time in 1953, and gaining the Triple Crown twice. Then between 1969 and 1979 Wales had an outstanding period, winning four Triple Crowns in a row and regularly crushing England. Indeed, in the amateur period Wales had the best record of any country in top British-European rugby, but since professionalism began in 1995 France, England and Ireland have beaten Wales more often than Wales has succeeded against them – a humbling thought.

When rugby union turned professional it became clear that Wales would have problems. Hitherto Welsh international players had usually played for Welsh clubs because they could compete in top level sport on equal terms while living at home and enjoying their star status in the community. Cardiff, Swansea, Newport and Llanelli had provided the majority of international players, but clubs like Neath, Pontypool, Bridgend, Aberavon and Pontypridd often competed strongly against them. But in 2003 the Welsh Rugby Union decided that only four (originally five) Welsh regions should compete at the top level.

This has not been popular with the loyal fans of the original spread of clubs. At the time of writing there is a gulf between the Welsh international XV, with three Triple Crowns in nine years, and the four regions (Blues, Dragons, Ospreys, Scarlets), who have yet to win trophies at the highest level despite their star-studded ranks. They no longer play against other Welsh clubs, which in the past could usually be guaranteed to give the original big clubs a hard time, but now form a separate second tier. The four regional clubs desperately need more popular support to generate funds; the consequence of failure is that top Welsh players are tempted to join richer English and French clubs. The Welsh Rugby Union and national coaches resent this, but the situation could well deteriorate further, in imitation of the position in soccer. In the meantime more and more players from outside, keen to gain experience, come to join the Welsh regions. In effect the men's game is forced to learn from women's rugby; when the women's international XV was chosen only from Welsh clubs, they did badly, but when the policy was dropped results immediately improved.

Although Wales have won the Grand Slam four times since

Despite the (usually controlled) violence on the rugby field, players' respect for the referee and spectator behaviour is generally better than in the world of soccer. Even English fans can mingle safely with Welsh fans, though their ears may burn. Unfortunately racist prejudice and abuse marred Welsh sport as elsewhere in the UK, but the problem seems much reduced, thanks to the successes of Welshmen like Colin Jackson and Nigel Walker, and visiting cricketers like Clive Lloyd, Majid Khan and Waqar Younis.

2004, and though in the World Cup Wales gained third place in 1987, the competition then remained barren for Wales until 2011, when a rejuvenated Welsh team reached the semi-final, losing to France by one point, the winners in turn losing to New Zealand by one point. The Welsh team came home to win the 2012 Grand Slam yet again. Pride went before a fall; a summer tour to Australia brought three Test defeats in a row, followed by more defeats against Southern hemisphere countries in the autumn and a defeat by Ireland. Then suddenly the weather changed: Wales beat France, Italy and Scotland and then thrashed a promising England team 30–3. The team provided the captain, Sam Warburton, and 14 others for the Lions' 2013 victorious summer tour of Australia.

Welsh international crowds are as passionate as ever, but the wonderful crowd singing which lasted into the 1950s has declined miserably with the virtual death of so many chapel congregations, where so many men had learnt to sing in harmony. The greatest Welsh international players are still cherished as heroes, and even in the most argumentative circles it might be agreed that Gareth Edwards was the greatest of all. His statue can be seen forever exercising his scrum-half skills in the St David's shopping arcade, Cardiff.

In cricket the anomalies outlined at the start of this chapter are particularly obvious. Cricket for England and Wales is administered by the England and Wales Cricket Board. The only Welsh county team, Glamorgan, plays in the English county championship. The club was formed in 1888, and finally joined the first-class counties in 1924, winning its first match and losing all the rest that season. For years Glamorgan vied with Northamptonshire for the wooden spoon, though matters improved under the captaincy of Maurice Turnbull, J.C. Clay and Wilfred Wooller. The county plays 'home' games in Welsh centres in and beyond Glamorgan, and recently the English national XI has begun playing 'home' Tests at Sophia Gardens, Cardiff (though a one-day match between England and New Zealand in 1976 was held at Swansea).

After WWII, in which Maurice Turnbull was killed, Glamorgan raised their game to win the County Championship for the first time in 1948 (subsequently in 1969 and 1997), and have defeated each of the major Test-playing countries at least once (Australia twice, in 1964 and 1968). In one-day games they have won the Sunday League three times. The record is respectable, but in recent years they have played in the second division of the County Championship, and the dismal summer of 2012 didn't helped the club's finances. Over the years some 13 Glamorgan players have been chosen for England, few reaching their best form, while others equally good were consistently overlooked or had their careers affected by World War II.

The fourth sport in which Wales has enjoyed international success is boxing, whose Welsh history goes back to bare-knuckle prize-fighting contests three centuries ago. Cardiff, Newport and the eastern industrial valleys have a long record of producing boxing champions at British, European and World levels. For men born in poverty, with limited education and destined to a grim life in coal-mine or steelworks, boxing gave the rare chance of escape, and so many tried it that boxing became part of the culture of Merthyr Tudful, the Rhondda and other Valleys communities.

Some of the most popular Welsh boxers never won a world championship but nevertheless became legends in the sport. My father was one of millions who sat by their radios in the small hours one night in 1937 and heard how the Tonypandy heavyweight Tommy Farr stood up against Joe Louis, the greatest boxer of his age, for 15 rounds in New York, only to lose on points. Johnny Owen, the Merthyr Matchstick, was so skinny he didn't look capable of fighting anyone, but he was a brilliant boxer, winning British and European bantamweight championships, only to be knocked out in his challenge for the world title in Los Angeles in 1980. He died in a coma six weeks later. His statue stands in his home town.

The history of world boxing titles is controversial, and for some decades has been farcical, since four American bodies all recognise their own world champions at each given weight, though some boxers may hold two or more versions at the same time. In 1916 the then controlling bodies in the UK and the USA agreed to recognise Jimmy Wilde as the world flyweight champion, but in 1914 another Rhondda boxer, Percy Jones, had already won the British version of the world flyweight title. He lost it after one successful defence and never fought Wilde.

Several Welsh world champions joined the ranks of boxing legend, while others are barely remembered. Jimmy Wilde was perhaps the greatest, a tiny man who in his youth could knock down men twice his size. He claimed to have fought over 700 times, though the official record allows a mere 149, of which he only lost four. Wilde found life difficult after leaving the ring and spent his last years in poverty. He died in 1969, aged

76, after suffering a brutal mugging four years earlier from which he never fully recovered. Other Welsh world champions include Freddie Welsh (lightweight 1914), Howard Winstone (featherweight 1968), Steve Robinson (featherweight 1993), Robbie Regan (bantamweight 1996), Barry Jones (super-featherweight 1997), Enzo Maccarinelli (cruiserweight 2006), Gavin Rees (welterweight 2007), and Nathan Cleverly (light-heavyweight 2011). Other Welsh boxers whose names still resonate include are Jim Driscoll, Dai Dower, Ronnie James, Cliff Curvis, Jack Petersen, Joe Erskine, Colin Jones and Eddie Thomas, manager of a legendary stable of Welsh boxers.

The most fearsome of modern Welsh boxers has undoubtedly been Joe Calzaghe, son of a Sardinian father and Welsh mother, born in London but living in Wales since the age of two, and identifying proudly with his adoptive country. Calzaghe was holder of the world super-middleweight and light-heavyweight championships for ten years until he retired in 2008. He is the only British world champion never to lose a fight between turning professional and retiring. At super-middleweight he actually succeeded,

From a rather special point of view, that of sports administration, a Welshman now almost forgotten made a unique contribution. He was John Graham Chambers, member of a wealthy Llanelli family, who was educated at Eton and Cambridge, where he gained a rowing Blue and later coached the Cambridge Eight for many years. In 1866 he established the organisation now known as the Amateur Athletic Association. In 1867 he drew up the so-called Marquess of Queensbury rules which govern boxing matches; in 1872 he arranged the first FA Cup final, and during his career instituted championships for billiards, boxing, cycling, wrestling and athletics. Such a varied career is hardly conceivable today!

after a series of fights, in winning all four versions of the world title at the same time, another rare feat.

In all four sports Wales has produced a good number of outstanding representatives and has a history of successes. Rugby League has glimmered promisingly on occasion, but has never succeeded in making its own space in Wales, though hundreds of players 'went North' between the wars, including some seventy internationals. The Welsh international League team were European champions in 1936, 1937 and 1938. There is a professional ice-hockey team in Cardiff, the Devils. Several world snooker champions have emerged from Wales; Ray Reardon, Terry Griffiths and Mark Williams. The country has produced one great golfer in Ian Woosnam and a victorious Ryder Cup captain, Dai Rees, the first Welshman to be voted British Sports Personality of the Year (1957). (Later Welsh recipients were David Broome in 1960, Joe Calzaghe in 2007 and Ryan Giggs in 2009). The one Welsh tennis player of note is Mike Davies. After reaching the men's doubles final at Wimbledon in 1960 Davies turned professional; he eventually became one of the game's most influential administrators and innovators. Many other games exist and flourish quietly with little public notice: hockey, basketball, croquet, for example (athletics and cycling are dealt with below). Darts produced one Welsh world champion, Leighton Rees in 1978; Kelly Morgan won the Commonwealth badminton singles in 1998, and Wales has produced top jockeys in Hywel Davies and Carl Llewellyn.

The Commonwealth Games of 1955 proved to be a major step-up for sport in Wales, especially with the provision of better facilities by the standards of the time. Since then there have been new stadia for rugby and football; several FA Cup finals were staged at the Millennium Stadium with huge success while Wembley was rebuilt, and Cardiff won much praise as a result. The Rugby World Cup was held in Wales in 1991 and the Ryder Cup at Newport in 2010.

Women's sporting activities in Wales suffer from the usual combination of attitudes best encapsulated as patronising neglect, especially by the media, and reluctance to abandon traditional patterns of social behaviour. Only three women's names appear among winners of BBC Wales's Sports Personality of the Year since 1954: Tanni Grey-Thompson (three times), Nicole Cooke and runner Kirsty Wade. Of the sports in which women have long had worldwide public recognition – tennis, athletics, swimming, gymnastics – only tennis gets guaranteed annual exposure on television, and in the past expensive facilities have rarely existed in Wales, at least outside Cardiff, though Swansea now offers excellent opportunities for swimming.

The best-established women's sports in Wales are certainly netball and hockey. Netball is entirely a women's game, and after leaving school more Welsh women play organised netball than any other sport. At senior level the Cardiff-based Celtic Dragons play in the English super-league; the national team plays regularly in international tournaments, and is currently ranked 14th in the world. There are also Welsh teams under-17 and under-19. There are numerous local netball clubs across the country.

Women's hockey was organised in Wales as early as 1897, only a year after the men's game. The Welsh Hockey Union lists 73 Welsh women's clubs distributed across the country, and international teams at under-16, under-18, under-21 and full international levels. There is no problem about Wales playing in international tournaments, and Welsh players can be chosen for the UK team in the Olympic Games.

In England women's football got away to a good start after

World War I, with many clubs and good support. Then the Football Association clamped down brutally, offering the usual sexist arguments, and though things have improved, media bias still makes life difficult for women footballers as opposed to tennis players and athletes. It must be hoped that the high profile of women's soccer at the 2012 Olympic Games will benefit the game in the United Kingdom. At the time of writing (summer 2013) any improvement is barely perceptible.

In Wales, organised women's football and rugby hardly existed before the 1980s, but times are changing. Traditionally schools have always offered gender-distinct games to girls, usually hockey and netball. Now girls and women are more ready to ask for equal entitlement to the games which, played by men, so fill the media. In rugby, before 1987, Welsh women only achieved international honours with a Great Britain XV, and there were hardly any regular teams functioning. But in 1991 Wales hosted the first ever Women's World Rugby Cup , defeated the South Africans on their own soil in 1994 by two Tests to one, and after a long series of defeats they finally beat England in 2009, winning their first Triple Crown in the process. Welsh women's soccer has been slower than rugby to become organised. A Welsh XI did not enter the FIFA Women's World Cup until 1999, or the European Women's Championship until 1995. A Welsh Premier Women's Football League wasn't organised until 2009; it now contains ten clubs.

Even at the highest level, women in all four team sports need to be either students or in employment. They have to practice when time allows and to pay a lot of their own expenses. This could be called a blessing in that it helps keep out the seamier side of professional male sport, but a curse because media support is so feeble (in Wales the BBC, S4C and such national papers as we have are equally at fault with the rest of the UK media), and finance is difficult. Admission to matches is usually free; clubs have to do much of their own fundraising, while at international level (except for netball) they share premises, websites etc., with men's games. All Welsh women's games and sports have to rely to an extent on grants from organisations such as SportWales and on fundraising.

There is no doubt that Welsh women's participation in sport is improving, not least thanks to SportWales, but also to the internet, which provides anyone interested with much information which used to be difficult to find. Promising young women are in training and achieving success in sports as different as swimming, gymnastics, judo and weightlifting. Both women and men in Wales can enjoy good facilities if they live in the right place, but local opportunities are severely limited in rural Wales.

The Olympic Games provide a unique opportunity for sports other than football to gain media attention. In recent decades, with the end of traditional prejudices against women running more than short distances, doing the pole vault or fighting, female Olympic sports now claim huge coverage, and it must be hoped that after 2012 they will not disappear back into the shadows cast by the Premier football league. Welsh athletes and other sportsmen and women have gained varying success over the years since the fourth Games of 1908. From the early Games to the close of the London Games of 2012, Welsh representatives in the UK team have won 23 Olympic gold medals, 14 silver and 22 bronze, missing out entirely in several Olympiads: 1924, 1928, 1936 and 1976. Admittedly twelve of the golds came in Games held between 1908 and 1932, when far fewer countries competed and before drugs and international politics became serious problems.

Readers looking at Welsh medallists' names may wonder how 'Welsh' some of these performers were. Obviously there are shades of Welshness. Take for example two names, the Cardiff swimmer Paulo Radmilović, who at London (1908), Stockholm (1912) and Antwerp (1920) won four gold medals in swimming and water polo, and David Jacobs, winner of a gold medal in the Stockholm Games of 1912. Jacobs was born in Cardiff but raised in London. Radmilović, on the other hand, was a Cardiff Bute Street boy who learned his swimming in the Glamorgan canal and the river Taff. By every sane standard Radmilović was Welsh. So is Colin Jackson, the first black athlete from Wales to win an Olympic medal (silver, 1988). Unlucky not to win gold, he is without doubt the finest Welsh track athlete to date.

Other notable Welsh Olympians are Irene Steer, first Welsh woman gold medallist in 1912, Tom Richards, silver in the 1948 marathon and the only Briton ever to win a marathon medal; Welsh rugby international Ken Jones, relay silver medallist in 1948; equestrian Sir Harry Llewellyn in 1952, Lynn Davies the long jumper, victorious at Tokyo in 1964 and Nicole Cooke, Tokyo winner of the women's road racing cycling gold and a superstar in her sport.

The London Olympics of 2012 brought special honours to Welsh sport. Dai Greene, world 400 metres hurdles champion for 2011, was chosen captain of the Great Britain athletics team, while Ryan Giggs, after a career outside world football contests, captained the Great Britain soccer team which had four other Welshmen in its squad. Nineteen-year-old Jade Jones of Flint became Wales's youngest ever Gold medallist in Taekwondo, while Geraint Thomas repeated his cycling team pursuit Gold of 2008. Seven medals for Welsh athletes was the best haul ever.

If sporting success be measured in gold, then Welsh

Paralympic athletes have stood closer to the summit of world sport than any other group of Welsh sportspeople. Tanni Grey-Thomspon's huge success over several Games, winning eleven racing golds, has been extraordinary. That and her other skills have brought her a life peerage; she took the oath in the House of Lords in both Welsh and English. Other Welsh paralympists have also done well. At Beijing in 2008 Great Britain won 42 golds – ten of them thanks to the Welsh team members. In particular swimmer Dave Roberts ran up four golds, bringing his lifetime total to eleven, equal to Grey-Thompson.

At the last moment of revising I discovered a memorial in Ammanford Civic Cemetery to a forgotten Welsh sportswoman. Edith Mair Leonard (her married name) died on 6 October 1970 aged 34, having swum the English Channel the previous year. The Channel Swimming Association names her as Mair Leonard of Wales; her time was 19 hours 45 minutes. Other Welsh women who have swum the Channel are Jenny James and Brenda Fisher.

In the 2012 Paralympics Welsh athletes were less successful than at Beijing, winning three gold medals, three silver and nine bronze. The Welsh element in the British team was weakened by injury to the remarkable cyclist Simon Richardson, badly hurt by a hit-and-run driver and thus unable to compete. The outstanding Welsh parathlete in 2012 was cyclist Mark Colbourne of Tredegar, with one gold and two silvers. In 2008 and 2010 both Welsh parathletes and able-bodied athletes have benefited from the government money and media publicity which saw British Olympic teams better prepared than ever before.

12. Looking *for* Welsh Pseudo-history

Just what, pray, is pseudo-history? Well, think Romulus and Remus, legendary founders of Rome. Think Noah and the Ark, or the Tower of Babel. Think King Alfred burning the cakes. Think Robert Bruce and the spider in the cave. Peoples have always told themselves stories about the past, especially about their own past, about their creation and their early history. Sometimes they are based on fact – both Alfred and Robert the Bruce were real men. Both can be legitimately credited with the renewal of their nations, but the cakes and the spider are folklore. Many stories, like that of Romulus and Remus, tell of the foundation of a city or a nation which supposedly derives its name from the founder. In fact, these men's names were invented from the original place-name. So Romulus 'explains' the name of Rome, and the story is romanticised by the motif of their adoption as babies by a she-wolf which suckled them.

In fact the Romans' foundation myth was more complicated. Although they believed that Rome had been founded in 753 BC, supposedly by Romulus, they also wanted to involve the legend of the city of Troy in their story, even though they believed that Troy had been destroyed by the Greeks in 1184 BC. The Trojan warrior Aeneas, according to legend, had escaped from Troy, and so further legends evolved which brought him eventually to Italy, to become the ancestor of Romulus and Remus.

Believe it or not, all this is surprisingly relevant to Welsh pseudo-history, even to 'real' history. The first surviving effort to write an extended British history is a ninth-century Latin text called *A History of the Britons*. The text has a preface which claims that the author had 'made a heap of all that he could find', which is perhaps the truest of all his assertions, since the work is garbled and the text varies from manuscript to manuscript. But clearly the author, who is conveniently but erroneously known as 'Nennius', had big ideas. To repeat all the variants would be dull in the extreme, but the essence is clear, and his ambition was considerable – much more than his short text justifies.

It's clear that other people had long been at work developing the stories that are piled up in this text. Indeed, the stories spread themselves across centuries: the origin of the British or Welsh people and their supposed history down to the Roman invasions, the story of Magnus Maximus, the British Roman emperor, the coming of the Saxons and the treasonous folly of Vortigern, Merlin and the battle of the red and white dragons, and above all, the feats of Arthur, king and emperor. To deal with all this material would need a book, so this chapter is confined to the first topic – Britain before the Romans. For Arthur, see chapter 8.

Britain, so 'Nennius' tells us, derives its name from Brutus, who is not only a descendant of Aeneas of Troy and relative of Romulus but also a descendant of Japheth, son of Noah! Thus Brutus the founder of Britain is descended not only from the Trojan Aeneas (himself of divine descent), he also has biblical ancestry. Not only that: Japheth's lineage went back to Adam son of God! So Britain's origins are doubly blessed with divine prestige both classical and Biblical, a unique combination in these origin stories.

Brutus's descendants, the Britons or Brythoniaid, i.e. the Welsh, were still here, but the land they controlled had shrunk dreadfully, so all the more need for a glorious ancestry to comfort them. This was the more glorious because another British Brutus produced by 'Nennius' was the brother of

Francus, Alamanus and Romanus, and therefore the British – Welsh – could claim relationship with the Franks (French), the Alemanni (Germans) as well of course as the Romans, not to mention the Trojans. The Welsh names Ffrainc, Almaen and Rhufain are clearly in the writer's imagination.

A History of the Britons was an important text – there are 35 surviving manuscripts – but in the early twelfth century, when Wales was being slowly chewed up by greedy Norman barons, a great writer of Latin seized on these and other stories. Fortified by his vivid imagination, Geoffrey of Monmouth wove it all into what looks like a seamless whole. Whether Geoffrey was Welsh, Breton, Norman or English we don't know for certain, but he surely had at least some grasp of the Welsh language. He passed off his work of sheer fiction as *The History of the Kings of Britain*, and it was published about 1136.

Geoffrey's book is an extraordinary farrago, which proved immensely popular. Versions of it soon appeared in English and French, while it was translated into Welsh three times, since it was much more exciting reading than the real but little-circulated Welsh chronicles of the time. The work is divided into twelve sections or books; the first three are derived from the *History of the Britons,* from

> It is at this point that we can relate the pseudo-history to real history. In the last days of Welsh independence, when Llywelyn ap Gruffudd was besieged in Snowdonia in 1282, Edward I's messenger, Archbishop John Pecham, attempted to persuade Llywelyn and his nobles to surrender. But they would have none of it. They told the archbishop that Gwynedd was part of the lands of Camber son of Brutus, which the Princes of Wales held by descent and by the confirmation of the Pope's legate. It was inalienable. Edward himself would certainly have seen himself as the descendant of Locrinus.

royal genealogies and from folk tales. Geoffrey tells of the wanderings of Brutus on his way to Britain and of his arrival and occupation of the island, of Queen Gwendolen, of Bladud of Bath, King Lear and his daughters, of the lawgiver Dunwallo Moelmutus and of King Lud. All quite fictional!

Brutus's wife bears him three sons, Locrinus, Albanactus and Kamber. Locrinus, the eldest, possessed the middle part of the island, called afterwards from his name, Loegria. Kamber, the youngest, had that part which lies beyond the river Severn called Cambria, while Albanactus possessed the northern country called Albania. The sons' names were of course invented as back-formations from the Welsh names Lloegr (England), Alban (Scotland) and Cymru, the Welsh name for the country and its people. If Geoffrey was not a Welshman, he was certainly familiar with the language.

Geoffrey cheerfully produced British king after British king, some apparently derived from the genealogies, to fill the gap between Brutus and the arrival of the Romans, famously including the tale of King Lear and his three daughters. The English as well as the Welsh loved to repeat Geoffrey's tales, which were eventually incorporated into the Elizabethan chronicles of Hall and Holinshed. From the second edition of 1587 Shakespeare took not only the plots of his 'real' history plays (from *Macbeth* and *King John* to *Henry VIII*) but *King Lear* and *Cymbeline*, both originally from Geoffrey.

Then Geoffrey wheels in the Romans, and after numerous complications mostly unwarranted by history, wheels them out again. They are followed by Saxon invaders, with spectacular tales of bribery, collusion and corruption – not to mention mass murder of British chieftains by treacherous Saxons, the Treachery of the Long Knives (*Brad y Cyllyll Hirion* in Welsh). The fantastic figure of Merlin prophesies the future and builds

Stonehenge. Then the greatest of the British kings appears – Arthur. Not content with having him vanquish the Saxons in the battles listed in the *History of the Britons*, Geoffrey carries him off to build an empire in continental Europe, only for him to be forced to return by the treachery of his nephew Mordred.

There were sceptics from the start. Geoffrey's English contemporaries, the chroniclers William of Malmesbury (d. 1143) and William of Newborough (b. 1136), both scorned the *History*, while Gerald of Wales (d. 1215) claimed that the very manuscript of the work conjured up demons, it was so mendacious. Not that Gerald was indifferent; he borrowed some of the stories, without acknowledgement. These sceptics were largely ignored; Geoffrey's work was widely copied, translated and rewritten in verse. This popularity came at the very time when chivalry and courtly love were becoming fashionable, first in the courts of Provence, then across much of Western Europe. Chivalry needed a hero – who better than Arthur and his followers, now his knights, who first save damsels in distress and then pursue the Holy Grail. These preoccupations were unknown to Geoffrey.

In its Welsh translations, Geoffrey's history was seen as the centre of a tripartite view of history. A late classical text attributed to a Trojan, Dares Phrygius, purporting to tell the story of the Trojan War, was translated into Welsh in the belief that it told of the distant ancestors of Brutus. This was seen as a preface to Geoffrey's work, while *The Chronicle of the Princes*, a genuine chronicle recounting Welsh history to the death of Llywelyn ap Gruffudd in 1282, was treated as the third part.

The atmosphere became heated when the Italian scholar Polydore Vergil came to England in 1501 and was appointed bishop of Bath and Wells. He soon started work on a major *History of England*. When it was published in 1535 the book enraged scholars in England by its fierce attack on Geoffrey's *History*. The great English antiquary John Leland immediately reasserted the glories of Arthur's imperial reign, and a veritable platoon of cultured Welshmen united to attack Polydore Vergil. Humfrey Lhwyd, a leading Welsh humanist and contributor to important scholarship about Wales, happily indulged a talent for abuse to defend Geoffrey. Vergil, he said, spoke 'sclandrous lies' from his 'gnarrynge and doggish mouthe'.

Humfrey Lhwyd, however, was cautious. In his *Cronica Walliae* he refers several times to Brutus as the common ancestor of the Welsh, and once to the division of the island between Camber, Locrinus and Albanactus, but other than that he showed little interest in Geoffrey's work. He is more noteworthy as a genuine historian; the *Cronica* is his version of Welsh medieval history from the seventh century to the end of the 13th, adapted by David Powel for *The Historie of Cambria* (1584), the first published history of Wales. We don't know what Llwyd thought of the most imaginative of all the apologists for the ancient history of Britain.

This was John Bale, bishop of Ossory in Ireland. In 1548 he published in Latin a work whose title translates as *A Catalogue of the most Important British Authors from Japheth for 3,618 year up to… 1547*. Bale had picked up another name to add to the genealogy of the supposed kings of Britain – Samothes. This man, so Bale believed, following an Italian writer, Annius of Viterbo, was another son of Japheth. Samothes had died in 2014 BC, but not before giving his name to the island of Britain, Samothea, and begetting the first of a long line of kings of the Celts, including King Bardus, from whom the bards drew their name. Both Bale and Leland gave special attention to the bards, who included Merlin and Taliesin, and even a number of the Welsh saints. Interest in the bards, especially in their role as supposed descendants of the Druids, would be greatly expanded in the 18th century, but Bale and Leland had already given it a good start.

The fictitious names of the early British kings spread like bacteria. Before 1600 the Welsh humanist and poet Edmwnd Prys was citing the name of Samothes in his bardic dispute with Wiliam Cynwal. A number of English scholars followed up and elaborated the story of Samothes, but during the 17th century more and more writers became doubtful, some omitting him and his kin altogether from their work, though they were far from dead. It was in Wales, however, that the pseudo-history would be kept alive most vigorously.

It would be a mistake to think that there was only one version of the pseudo-history. Welsh scholars had seized upon the figure of Gomer, son of Japheth and brother of Samothes, as a figure of the greatest interest. Unlike Samothes, Gomer is mentioned in the Bible, and according to the Jewish historian Josephus, writing in the first century AD, the descendants of Gomer lived in Galatia – which really was the home of a Celtic tribe to whom St Paul addressed one of his letters. The English antiquarian William Camden, writing in 1586, linked Gomer with a European tribe, the Cimbri, and with the Cymry, the Welsh-language name for the Welsh people.

This opened another explosive field – pseudo-linguistics. What language would Gomer have spoken? Hebrew of course. Now the Welsh word for the Welsh language is *Cymraeg*. How else to explain this word but as *Gomeraeg*, the language of Gomer? Thus Welsh must be descended from Hebrew! It took no time at all even for the major Welsh scholars Siôn Dafydd Rhys and John Davies to make this association and start looking for common linguistic roots. Not every scholar accepted the theory; some preferred Geoffrey of Monmouth's derivation of *Cymraeg* from *Cam-Roeg* – crooked Greek. Only the first and greatest of serious Celtic scholars, Edward Lhuyd (d. 1709), took no notice of this nonsense, but his outstanding work in Celtic philology, *Archaiologia Britannica* (1707) was less exciting than the wild fantasies of the past, which were to hold sway in Wales for a good while yet.

During the 17th century almost all the pseudo-history of Wales is to be found in English or Latin texts. One, not published until 1719 but written over a century earlier, was the *History of Great Britain* by the Radnorshire barrister John Lewis of Llynwene (d. 1616). Lewis was not only utterly credulous, he was happy to expand on Bale's farrago of pre-Roman kings. Whether his work was widely known before its posthumous appearance is not entirely clear, but his account of Samothes was certainly taken up by at least one Welsh writer, as we shall shortly see.

Among men less credulous than John Lewis the pseudo-history still simmered away through the rest of the 17th century. Even William Wynne, who edited the *History of Cambria* of 1584 under his own name in 1697 as *The History of Wales*, was reluctant to let Brutus disappear altogether. He devoted thirty pages of his preface weighing the evidence for and against Geoffrey of Monmouth, and was so reluctant to let go of his work that he persuaded himself that something at least of the truth must survive among the ruins of the Brutus story.

The pseudo-history was given a new boost by the publication in 1703 of Paul-Yves Pezron's history of the Celts, soon translated from French into English. In particular this remarkable work gave new life to the Druids and quickly infected Wales. In 1723 Henry Rowlands published his history of Anglesey, *Mona Antiqua Restaurata*, in which he gave considerable and uncritical space to the Druids, naturally enough considering their genuine connection to the island in pre-Roman times. The second edition of Rowlands' work by Henry Owen, published in 1766, expatiated at further length on the Druids. Pezron can be considered the father of the 18th century cult of Druidism, which assumed ever more extraordinary status as the century went by, especially when taken up by Iolo Morganwg, whose pseudo-history deserves a whole chapter.

Meanwhile Gomer and Brutus were given new life in the Welsh language in 1716. The Teifiside Anglican priest, Theophilus Evans printed his *Drych y Prif Oesoedd* ('The Mirror of the First Ages') at Shrewsbury in that year. In 1740 he brought out a much enlarged edition, by which time the number of literate Welsh people was increasing rapidly, and the book became a firm favourite for more than a century, went into many editions and was translated into English.

Theophilus Evans wrote a sturdy Welsh prose which carried his readers fluently along the wild shores which he described. Ignoring Samothes, he begins his story with Gomer and the Tower of Babel, when the peoples could no longer speak the same language to each other. He sweeps his readers along with his enthusiasm:

> I am sure that this is the undoubted truth, that Gomer is the absolute and certain ancestor of the Welsh. Because our very name, *Cymero*, declares it. Whence comes that name but from *Gomero*? *Cymru* but from *Gomeri*? It would be a waste of time to prove anything so self-evident.

Gomer and those who speak the same tongue eventually reached the island of Britain, 'where they lived I know not how long' until Brutus came among them. Then, having indulged in some linguistic theories of his own, Theophilus moves on immediately to the arrival of the Romans over a thousand years later because, as he glibly explains, surely with a touch of irony:

> It is not because I am ignorant of the Chronicle of the Kings of Wales [i.e. Geoffrey's *History*] that I tell nothing of their rule, but because many learned men doubt the truth of what has been told about them. In any case that material is largely trivial.

This intriguing apology is omitted in the expanded version of the *Drych* which Theophilus published in 1740. Instead he expanded on his linguistic theories and savagely attacked William of Malmesbury, who had been the first authority to cast doubts on Geoffrey's *History*. Then he simply jumps to the Romans without further ado.

Before 1740, however, other history books in Welsh had been published. Simon Thomas of Hereford brought out his little *Llyfr Gwybodaeth y Cymro* (The Welshman's Book of Knowledge), reissued in 1723 and later editions as *Hanes y Byd a'r Amseroedd* (A History of the World and the Times), but in spite of many other weaknesses Thomas's work ignored the pseudo-history entirely. He wisely preferred to give an account of the solar system and the world as he understood them, but his history of Christianity involved sustained and savage criticism of Roman Catholicism.

Ignored by Theophilus Evans, Samothes was still in limbo, but not dead. In 1728 a nonconformist preacher and weaver, Thomas William of Mynydd Bach in the Tywi valley, brought out his remarkable *Oes-Lyfr*. Whereas Theophilus Evans, in his second edition of the *Drych*, had indulged himself to the extent of 362 pages, Thomas William's *Oes-Lyfr* (Book of Ages), published in 1728, only extends to 92 pages. The *Drych* could not easily have been afforded by humbler folk, but the *Oes-Lyfr* (sixpence for the second edition of 1768) was much cheaper. Though his work was brief, Thomas William was seriously ambitious. His title-page promises a Biblical directory, dealing with the prophets and the books of the Old and New Testaments. Then follows his catalogue of the kings and princes of Britain and Wales; he brought the 1768 edition up to the death of George III. Finally he describes all the most remarkable happenings in their reigns.

The pseudo-history of Britain is given respectful attention, without doubts or quibbles:

> This Island was once called Samothea, after Samothes (as some say) son of Japheth, son of Noah, who first dwelt here about fourteen hundred years after the Flood.

He moves swiftly on to King Bardus, after whom the bards were named, and to consult whom the wise men of Athens would send for advice when unable to agree among themselves. Naturally these bards dwelt in Anglesey. Thomas William then digresses to defend the pseudo-history against the cavils of hostile Englishmen, and cites a row of authorities to justify his views, including John Bale.

Thomas William repeats as many of the fantastic stories about Brutus and his successors as he can find room for – the founding of New Troy (London), the vicious Queen Gwendolen and her son King Madog, who was devoured by wolves when Samuel was a prophet in Israel. He treated his own people brutally, but his successor Membyr (founder of the city of Oxford) was even worse; he was so consumed with sexual lust that he gave up his wives and concubines in favour of animals. It's worth reminding ourselves that Thomas William, himself a keen Christian and devotional writer, was publishing this startling material at a propitious time for Welsh authors. The Society for the Promotion of Christian Knowledge has founded a number of schools and was paying to send Welsh Bibles and books of devotion to Wales. Griffith Jones of Llanddowror was launching his peripatetic schoolteachers to bring godly literacy to the Welsh people. But the pseudo-history lingered on in reprints. The third reprint of *Oes-Lyfr*, published about 1822 at a shilling, was updated by an unknown writer, still contained all the material of the first edition a century earlier.

Theophilus Evans's *Drych y Prif Oesoedd* stayed in print fairly regularly into the 19th century and achieved the dignity of a scholarly edition in the early 20th century as a work of literature, not history. Only with the appearance of several serious histories of Wales during the 19th century, culminating in the work of Sir John Edward Lloyd published in 1911, did the pseudo-history fade away, leaving only the fanciful Druidic vestments of the Gorsedd of Bards, worn during their ceremonies at the National Eisteddfod every year, as a last souvenir. At its worst the pseudo-history had encouraged rich levels of credulous fantasy, especially about a past so much of which was beyond recovery. At its best, it had given pride of tradition to a people sorely deprived of their own history by circumstances beyond their control.

Appendix: Further Reading

Several of the chapters have no simple routes to further reading; my information on a single theme may have come from many sources. But the following will certainly help for some subjects, especially with the aid of their bibliographies.

For Welsh history in general, begin with J. Graham Jones, *The History of Wales: A Pocket Guide* (Cardiff, 1998). For Cardiff, John Davies, *Cardiff: A Pocket Guide* (Cardiff, 2002). For the Welsh language, start with Janet Davies, *A History of the Welsh Language* (Cardiff, 1999 and reprints). For castles, churches and houses, Simon Jenkins, *Wales: Churches, Houses, Castles* (Penguin, 2008). For castles alone, John Kenyon, *The Medieval Castles of Wales* (Cardiff, 2010) or Gerald Morgan, *Castles in Wales* (Tal-y-bont, 2008). For churches, T.J. Hughes, *Wales's Best One Hundred Churches* (Seren, 2006). For houses, there is an admirable survey of all kinds of houses in Wales in *Introducing Houses of the Welsh Countryside* by Richard Suggett and Greg Stevenson (Tal-y-bont, 2010). For literature, Dafydd Johnston, *The Literature of Wales: a Pocket Guide* (Cardiff, 1994). For Welsh names, begin with T.J. Morgan and Prys Morgan, *Welsh Surnames* (Cardiff, 1985). For sport, Martin Johnes, *A History of Sport in Wales: a Pocket Guide* (Cardiff, 2005). The pseudo-history of Wales is a vast quagmire of a subject, but a good point of departure is Karen Jankulak's *Geoffrey of Monmouth* (Cardiff, 2010).